Poor Man's Provence

ALSO BY RHETA GRIMSLEY JOHNSON

America's Faces

Good Grief: The Story of Charles M. Schulz

Georgia

Poor Man's Provence

Finding Myself in Cajun Louisiana

RHETA GRIMSLEY JOHNSON

FOREWORD BY BAILEY WHITE

NewSouth Books
Montgomery | Louisville

NewSouth Books
P.O. Box 1588
Montgomery, AL 36102

Copyright © 2008 by Rheta Grimsley Johnson
All rights reserved under International and Pan-American Copyright Conventions. Published in the United States by NewSouth Books, a division of NewSouth, Inc., Montgomery, Alabama.

Library of Congress Cataloging-in-Publication Data

Johnson, Rheta Grimsley, 1953-
Poor man's Provence : finding myself in Cajun Louisiana / Rheta Grimsley Johnson.
p. cm.
Includes bibliographical references.
ISBN-13: 978-1-58838-218-4
ISBN-10: 1-58838-218-4
1. Cajuns—Louisiana—Social life and customs. 2. Louisiana—Social life and customs. 3. Johnson, Rheta Grimsley, 1953—-Homes and haunts—Louisiana—Henderson. 4. Henderson (La.)—Biography. 5. Cajuns—Louisiana—Henderson—Biography. 6. Cajuns—Louisiana—Henderson—Social life and customs. 7. Henderson (La.)—Social life and customs. I. Title.
F380.A2J64 2007
917.63'40464—dc22

2007041010

Design by Randall Williams

Printed in the United States of America
by the Maple-Vail Book Manufacturing Company

Acknowledgments

The poem "Yellow" by Robert Service is used by permission of his estate. I also want to thank Chelsey Reid, Tony Salmon, and Annie Bates, all of whom encouraged me at different times to finish this little book. Editors Suzanne La Rosa and Randall Williams were steadfastly patient and wise, and I am grateful to them as well. The names of the children in the chapter called "Toolshed Reading Club" have been changed to protect the innocent. — R. G. J.

For Don, who loves it, too.

Contents

FOREWORD

JUNE BAILEY WHITE

W ho has not dreamed at some low point in career or personal life of simply tossing it all aside and running away to a completely different world? Loose the fetters of bitter disappointment, creeping disillusionment, or just the wearing grind of the same old same old and a whole new self might spring forth—more insightful, talented, purposeful, and capable.

Writers have that dream.

Forget the hackneyed "Write what you know!" When deadlines loom, editors grow peevish, and the native air stagnates, a writer longs for untried territory. All the better if the new place is one she loves, with good music, great food, entertaining people, and a deep and mysterious swamp.

From the fine old travel books—*The Canterbury Tales, Humphry Clinker, Robinson Crusoe*—to the new books by Frances Mayes and Peter Mayle, there is a long and honored tradition of escape in literature. However, some of the worst writing in the world has gushed in purple ink from writers in that foolish flush of first love with a place. In the heat of passion it is easy to lose perspective and reason, and just rave on.

Like those overlayered paintings of cottages in sunlit glades, with a babbling brook alongside, and flowers from every climate zone in riotous full bloom, books about newly beloved places are often unrealistic, inaccurate, or just plain wrong. The skeptical reader will soon wonder, and rightly so: Don't spiders live in that thatched roof, and isn't the house sitting in the flood plain of that brook?

Writing too cool, however, is equally odious. These are the books where the worldly writer insinuates himself into a provincial culture and settles down to observe the natives with detachment and reserve. With clever irony and an omniscient voice he writes about their cunning ways, their endearing dialect, and their charming ignorance. Drawn in by a smooth prose style and a promise of escape, the poor reader soon finds himself squirming and ill at ease, feeling like an uninvited guest, ushered in by the writer to a place where neither is welcome.

In *Poor Man's Provence*, Rheta Grimsley Johnson manages something that is difficult to do in life and in writing: she balances true love with a level head.

She writes eloquently about real friendship, hot French bread, and a spider wedding. But she does not leave out junk cars, trash in the ditches, and pit bull dogs chained to pecan trees. Azalea bushes die in her yard, but neighborhood children flock to her tool shed to read books and sprinkle glitter. She admits early to being a tourist. She says, "Living for a decade in a place doesn't give me the right to report as a native." She

---

BAILEY WHITE *is the bestselling author of* Mama Makes Up Her Mind *and* Sleeping at the Starlite Motel. *A south Georgia elementary school teacher, Bailey White became one of America's most beloved essayists by reading her work aloud in her slow drawl on National Public Radio's* All Things Considered.

vows that she has learned more from her neighbors than about them.

Insightful without being nosy, clever without being smug, funny without poking fun, this is one of those welcoming books, like some of the Acadian households Johnson describes, where everyone feels at home. Both her readers and the people she writes about will be comfortable, well fed, highly entertained, and happy they came to poor man's Provence.

PREFACE

Who would have figured a wild boar hunt would be a bore? Not the Atlanta newspaper editor who noticed an advertisement for one in *Soldier of Fortune* magazine. He felt inspired and sent me packing. That's how editors work it. They have the bright idea, and the reporter does the work. Never mind it's almost always impossible for a writer to execute another's inspiration. That creative obstacle never occurs to most editors, even the good ones.

You would expect, at the least, to feel *something* at a wild boar hunt. Invigorated. Disgusted. Something. I went through the motions, but it wasn't really my kind of story. The result ran buried in the sports section, and the writing was lackluster at best. Not my proudest journalistic moment. Perhaps I should have seen the writing on the wall and begged off, which didn't win brownie points with a boss, but could be done. But, no, thank goodness I accepted the assignment with a grin, packed my grip and headed to south Louisiana. I went. I went because that's what you do when you're on salary and still believe—or try to—that no matter how stupid a story idea might seem, somehow a good enough writer can make it matter to the reader, can mine deep for real meaning in what, on the surface, may seem an insipid or insignificant idea.

Mostly I went because the hog hunt was in Louisiana.

Louisiana was always good for a story. In the past, I'd had wonderful reporting luck there, which usually means bad luck for somebody else. I'd covered a raucous, flag-waving David Duke rally, back when that blond, surgically-tailored Ku Klux Klansman was running for governor against former Governor Edwin Edwards. The all-time best political bumper sticker derived from that campaign, when Duke gave smarmy Edwards a run for his money: VOTE FOR THE CROOK; IT'S IMPORTANT.

I'd also written about an alligator's funeral in Ponchatoula, and had interviewed the geriatric stripper Chris Owens on Bourbon Street. I'd had lunch and a long talk with the former singing governor, Jimmie Davis, just days before his hundredth birthday.

Louisiana, this nation's funky Xanadu, almost always meant sexy copy.

My destination this time, for the wild boar hunt, was five hundred miles from Atlanta, across the bottom of Mississippi and over the steamy Atchafalaya Swamp of south Louisiana, smack dab in the heart of Cajun Country, near its unofficial capital, Lafayette. The Louisiana legislature, highbrows, and local television stations call the area Acadiana, which sounds a tad prissy.

I think back now to that fateful trip, one of thousands I have made in three decades as a newspaper reporter and columnist. I've been to pretty, melon-colored places like Key West in Florida and Mystic Seaport in Connecticut. In the name of good journalism, I've rafted the whitewater of the Middle Fork of the Salmon River in a pristine part of Idaho. From a graceful old front porch on Fishers Island in the Long Island Sound, I've watched billowing sails of boats as they cruised the Atlantic seaboard. I've slept late in a suite at Richmond's grand Jefferson Hotel.

I've been privileged to see lush, grand, beguiling places, all in the name of duty. And of course I've seen some fiercely ugly ones, too. More of those, really—news most often happens in the god-forsaken parts of the world, the slums and ghettos and back alleys. To paraphrase one of my favorite writers, Raymond Chandler, working for a newspaper is a lot like taking a glass-bottomed boat ride in a sewer. I had toured my share of sewers.

Never before had I returned from any assignment determined to return, to buy property and to spend time with the natives. Not once had I become so instantaneously hooked on the people and the culture that I invested my own dollars and ultimately a decade of my time in repeat trips to the same destination.

If I had operated as usual I'd have gone straight home to my computer to rhapsodize about Cajun Country in print. I would have related my fresh impressions to the readers, stuck a few personal photographs and souvenir brochures in a scrapbook and soon forgotten about it—both the place and the scrapbook. I must have three dozen half-filled scrapbooks. Best case: I might have remembered it fondly and perhaps forever, filed it away under pleasant memories and memorable locations.

But this was no typical work trip. What happened in Louisiana that hog hunt weekend was what some people and all the self-help books call "life-altering." Life-altering, a.k.a. life-enhancing, myth-shattering, epiphanous. I would redis-cover the value of verities in this workaday, swampy, unlikely land. I would recall vivid yet forgotten lessons from my south Georgia childhood, where on the banks of Spring Creek my grandfather chanted in a singsong baritone as he cooked up the day's catch. He was the Julius Caesar of instant gratifica-tion. He fished, he caught, he cooked, he ate. The cornmeal for frying he kept in a sack in his truck. This was natural order. That immediacy, the gratification without delay or buffer, he knew and appreciated. His habit of truly living off the land, not to mention the water, had thrilled me as a child, had touched something in my soul, had seemed oh-so right. It still does. My grandfather left this life owing nobody, with a little change to spare. He was rich while he lived because he didn't require much. And he didn't measure wealth in dollars. On his mental ledger, wealth was toted in another way. Having plenty meant free time for sunsets savored from the porch, ripe melons on dewy mornings, and energy for working hard with some left over to hunt or fish.

The people I met in deep Cajun Country were the same way—at least in their definition of abundance. They would help me determine once and for all what is most important in life— the woods, the water, time before money, friendship and family before all else. The Cajuns value good music, full bellies, hard work, and each other. The Cajun people with whom we became friends have simple needs, are amazingly resourceful, and seem never to lose their way. Hank Williams—a Cajun hero, by the way—once wrote a song about being lost on the river, the river of life. It's not one of his best-known songs—maybe because he sang it as a duet with his tone-deaf wife, Audrey—but it's one of my favorites. The metaphor is so simple it's stunning. Life is a river, with all a river's attributes and obstacles. So many of us get lost on that meandering river, the river of life. We founder in the shoals of modernity, sink to our necks in technology, drown under the weight of too many possessions. We live to work. In Cajun Country, people work to live. And live they do, gloriously and riotously. They don't only suck crawfish heads; they suck all there is to get out of this life.

Could it be that simple? Was the secret to a happy life to

live happily? I would spend the next ten years exploring that thesis, digging at our good times in southwest Louisiana like an archaeologist probes a site. The celebrated Cajun *joie de vivre*—which Webster's defines as keen or buoyant enjoyment of life—was layered but not complicated, deep but not distant. What you need to be happy is not in a catalogue or on a shelf. It's been beside, beneath, and around you all the while. It all seems so obvious now. But setting out that beautiful fall day in September 1996, to find one more story, to please an editor back in an Atlanta cubicle, to pay the mortgage and buy yet another object to dust, I could not have imagined the lessons I was about to learn, the people I would come to know and eventually to love. First, though, before the romance could begin, there was the boar hunt . . .

Poor Man's Provence

Blood, Guts, and a Bill

Boarbusters Hunting Lodge was in the middle of fifteen hundred wooded acres, with eighty of them enclosed by a tall hurricane fence to make a glorified hog pen. Early on the appointed morning I joined a half dozen young men who were—as they described it—"pumped," visibly hung-over, yet still eager to stalk the unsuspecting razorback. One of the boys, Michael of Baton Rouge, was to be married in two weeks. The hog hunt was his bachelor party, a last hurrah in the wild with old friends. Even a fool would get the symbolism.

From our friends, save us all.

A dainty but tough and talkative woman named Sissy Hall met us with a wry smile and explained the Boarbusters ground rules. Thin, with wild blond curls and fine features, she was the unlikely looking half of the couple who owned the hog hunting compound. Bruce Hall, her husband, was away on an alligator hunt, she explained matter-of-factly. That left Sissy in charge. She was up to it.

"Find yourself a tree, a little one," she said, merry eyes mocking us. "You can't shinny up a big tree. You don't have to go real high, just high enough to be out of their reach."

Somehow I suspected she wasn't kidding. Her own skinny legs were scarred from scaling trees to avoid mad hogs.

Prospective groom Michael and his friends strapped on holsters with big handguns to back up their bows and arrows.

The group had spent the previous night in the Boarbusters lodge—a rustic cabin full of mounted trophies with spooky glass eyes—drinking beer and dreaming of killing serious hogs. Sissy explained the hunt was free if you didn't go home with a hog in your cooler. If you bagged a non-trophy, or so-called "meat" hog, you paid $165. A trophy boar would cost you $325 and a super trophy boar $495. Exactly what constituted a "trophy boar" and a "super boar" never was clear to me. Perhaps it was left to the discretion of the Boarbusters management, who surely kept close track of the squealing inventory and made such critical designations.

On a weekly basis, Bruce Hall captured wild hogs in the swamp, using human handcuffs to bind the boars' legs after his pit bulls pinned them to the ground. That sounded more like the real hog hunt, if you asked me, which, of course, nobody did.

The no-nonsense Sissy and her young son transported us by four-wheelers from the lodge to the hunting ground, where we joined our guides, David Fontenot and Paul Manuel. For an hour or so the serious young men noiselessly led our party this way and that through hardwoods and spiky palmetto, making the eighty-acre pen seem like an endless wilderness. Nobody talked. We walked and walked.

We stumbled along through the woods, the ground littered with black muscadines, constantly slapping at super-trophy-sized mosquitoes. The only word for the forced hike was "boring." We were walking in big circles, which soon enough became clear even to the uninitiated. Just as I was considering suggesting a mutinous picnic, we reached a bunch of snoring hogs, the advertised wild boars. One silent guide motioned for the bow hunters to decide who got the first shot. A boy named Brady from Baton Rouge seized the moment and unsheathed his arrow.

The guide then began poking at a sleeping razorback with a stick, jabbing and jumping back, jabbing and jumping back, like a child trying to wake a sleeping parent. He kept at it until every last one of the groggy hogs was awakened. The hogs grunted in unison, rose one by one and began, reluctantly, scattering into the thicket. The fearless hunter took aim. His arrow flew.

An amazing thing happened then. Brady's single arrow hit one hog, came out the other side and flew right on into another boar. Brady had wounded not one, but two hogs, raising his bill from zero to $330 in an instant. Brady looked amazed, proud, finally chagrined. You could hear him adding up the damage in his head. At this point he must have wished he and his friends had opted to buy the groom drinks and a night out instead of a day of boar hunting. One shot had just about exhausted the entire bachelor party budget.

A guide straddled one of the dying pigs and unsheathed his knife to finish the job the arrows only began. "Anybody else want to do it?" he asked, remembering his manners. He showed us all how to stab the boar in the heart, but nobody took him up on the offer.

As if on cue, Sissy appeared from nowhere on her four-wheeler. The guides quickly loaded the vehicle—one pig in front, the other in back—and Sissy carefully tied down both bloody carcasses with elastic straps. She roared away with the fresh kill. I might forget a lot of things in this life, but never the sight of the diminutive woman, blond curls flying in the breeze, making the dead-hog run through the woods.

We tramped about the pen for a few more hours, startling the wild—at least wildly irritated—hogs whenever we ran upon them. The guides seemed to know about where to look. The possibilities were not endless, the compound enclosed, as it was, by fence. Nobody seemed wild to make another expensive kill.

The wild boar hunt ended with a whimper back at the lodge. Exhausted, we sat in the shade and watched Sissy dress the hogs. She had hung the two of them on a scaffold with a hoist, something like a mechanic would use to lift a car engine. Each dangling hog must have outweighed the petite Sissy by two hundred pounds.

She made quick work of it. The hogs had long rips in their stomachs, and innards spilled onto a concrete apron. We sat and watched in wonder as Sissy hosed away the blood and guts.

A Queen Fit for a Boat

I had seen Cajun Country before, briefly. I had been once to the famous Crawfish Festival in Breaux Bridge, a three-day bacchanalia of food, drink, and music. Thousands attend. By midday on festival Saturday everyone is wading in ankle-deep crawfish shells, feeling campy and dangerously devil-may-care. Such an extravaganza is fun, but only serves up culture in pint-sized, stereotypical bites. You leave thinking you know something about the folks and their ways, but you have only been fed a pre-packaged snack. You've eaten, danced, perhaps even bought a handmade Cajun accordion. You've been teased, not satisfied.

In 1996, I knew precious little about the area, truth be told. I knew that I loved shrimp étoufée and Tabasco, and I loved crossing the nearly twenty miles of causeway between Baton Rouge and Lafayette. That impressive expanse of bridge puts you directly above, and in the middle of, the Atchafalaya Swamp. You can see the watery oasis from a distance, the way astronauts look down on earth. Its colors depend on the season. In the springtime the cypress and willows seem an unbroken ocean of apple green. In the late fall and winter the cypress is rusty red against a bright blue water and sky. The causeway is the threshold of an eerily enchanted place where water rises and recedes on a whim, where sugar is a crop, and French the language of familiarity. Until that causeway was built in the early 1970s, most of Cajun Country was truly remote, nigh inaccessible. With completion of the bridge began an accelerated assimilation of Cajuns into the greater American culture, a process that had started with World War II and the draft. In reverse, with the bridge, came a steady pilgrimage of tourists who wanted to see what the fuss over French-speaking Louisiana was all about.

The wild hog hunt with its hung-over participants hadn't lasted half a day. Don, my husband, had made the long trip to Louisiana with me. At the time he was teaching journalism at the University of Alabama at Birmingham and could steal a long weekend here and there. He was especially willing to accompany me when the story involved Louisiana, a state he already loved and knew pretty well; he had attended Louisiana State University for a while and, long ago, lived with a brother in New Orleans. As I had secretly hoped, the hog hunt assignment was over quickly, and my deadline on the resulting story was a week away. That left the rest of the weekend free for exploring. Maybe now, I thought, I'd see more of Cajun Country than the view from the bridge.

Don and I have been drawn to water all of our lives. We eddy up to any old shore. Don grew up on the Mississippi Gulf Coast in Moss Point, a picturesque little town near Pascagoula. There was always an outboard motor in the trunk of his father's car. For that matter, there was an outboard motor in the trunk of most cars. Boats you could rent. But everyone owned, and traveled with, his own motor. Never could tell when you might need one. It was that kind of life.

As an adult newspaper man, Don has lived in San Francisco, Corpus Christi, and in Natchez on that tenuous high bluff above the Mississippi River. It was no accident that his newspaper jobs always landed him near the water. You might say he planned his journalism career around it.

I was a happy toddler in Pensacola, Florida. Some of my first memories are of Coke-bottle-green waves and sugar-white sand on Santa Rosa Island, and of my father water skiing on the Gulf of Mexico. Daddy took a job transfer when I was seven, and, after that, I grew up in landlocked Montgomery, Alabama. Even as kids, my sister and I knew we were trading down when we heard we were moving from Pensacola to Montgomery. On moving day we cried buckets on the two-lane drive between the towns, fearing our days of building fairy-tale sand castles and riding the waves were over forever. It was a long ride.

I've tried to make up for my father's fate and job transfer the rest of my life.

Whenever my own job situation would allow it, I too have lived on or near the water, any old water: the Mississippi Sound, the Tennessee River, the Little Tallapoosa River in Georgia. My vacations typically involve some bucking boat or another and, more often than not, end in disasters worthy of film treatment. I have sat on the Gulf of Mexico with a sailboat's broken tiller in my hand, wondering aloud what kind of fool calls a boat trip a vacation. I've cussed my own questionable urges when water, gas, and beer all ran short at the same time, between marinas, on an open pontoon boat on the brand new Tennessee-Tombigbee Waterway the year the waterway was completed. Six of us made that trip, the whole four hundred and fifty waterway miles between Counce, Tennessee, and Mobile, Alabama. We somehow remained friends.

Don and I are like most couples. We disagree on a few things, but our weakness for anything to do with water is communal. We have taken freighter voyages across the Atlantic and canoe trips down Mississippi's Leaf River. We get to our fall

campsites on Pickwick Lake on a seriously overloaded skiff.
We even love the look of junked boats strewn about the yard.
Or maybe it's just that we're very used to the look of junked
boats strewn about the yard. We certainly agree that any time
spent on water prolongs life. It's a fun fact.

So that bright day in 1996, without much discussion, we
drove from the bloody Boarbusters compound back to the
Lafayette motel where we'd slept. We washed the morning's
muddy hog hunt from our bodies and minds. Then we got right
back in the car and headed straight to the levee that defines
the swamp, to check out the boats and quaint landings along
its cusp.

THE ATCHAFALAYA IS THE largest river overflow swamp in all
of North America and the largest contiguous forested wetland
in the Mississippi River Alluvial Plain. I read that somewhere
and am not all that sure what it means. But in plainer words,
there's gracious plenty water. Even what looks like land—green
expanses of water hyacinths and hydrilla—can be water. In
years to come, that hyacinth-and-hydrilla blanket would fool
our dog Mabel time and time again. She'd jump from the
boat onto what she assumed was terra firma, only to take a
surprise swim.

Don, who lives to hunt ducks, literally smelled the possibilities.

From Ville Platte and Boarbusters, we headed southeast,
to the Atchafalaya Basin, which you reach only by driving
through a workaday town called Henderson.

Henderson may well be the funkiest little town in Louisiana. It may be the homeliest town in all America, if you don't
count Peoria or Detroit, which I don't because they are cities.
But, then, you don't always fall in love because of good looks.

Sometimes personality trumps beauty.

Henderson is junky, unplanned, littered, but interesting. It may be the spiritual home of the wrecked automobile. There are more junked cars in the town than there are trees. Yard after yard, vacant lot after lot, you pass car graveyards—fascinating collections of totaled, annihilated heaps, their windshields splintered like varicose veins, sides crumpled like aluminum foil, wheel wells resting precariously on cinderblocks. Neighboring towns have their giant live oaks strung with Spanish moss—which, by the way, isn't Spanish and isn't moss—but Henderson has its abandoned cars. The town was a sugarcane field until relatively recently. Farmers had long ago clipped it clean of forest. All the better to store wrecked cars.

The town wasn't founded until after the Great Flood of 1927, when the soaked Cajun swamp-dwellers sought higher ground. After the flood, a lot of the trappers, fishermen, hunters and other swamp-dwellers who preferred to live in the Atchafalaya were forced by nature to move to the high, dry side of the levee, thus creating Henderson.

And on the eighth day, in a frivolous mood, God created manufactured housing. There are trailers of every description in Henderson, plus some that defy description. There is no stigma attached to trailer-living here; many consider it a social promotion to move from a small house to a larger double-wide. Even Henderson's city hall is housed in a double-wide in an uncharacteristically neat park that's also the repository for most of the town's few trees.

Henderson's main road, which runs about two miles from the interstate exit to the levee, is flanked for half its distance by a big, weed-infested drainage ditch. When the ditch is full of water, which is often, the litter in it floats. Plastic drink bottles, beer cans, potato chip bags, and cigarette cartons all rise, flanking the town's signature street with a soggy, 7-Eleven selection of refuse.

On the plus side, Henderson's prevailing architecture is the simple, 1950s-style frame house, the kind built before families thought they had to live in overwrought brick monstrosities too big for their lots, back when homeowners simply cut their grass instead of landscaping their yards. There is a nice, nostalgic feel about the bungalows and shotgun houses, many topped with metal roofs and kept neat as pins. Best of all, there is a work boat in almost every Henderson yard, and after a poor crawfishing season, many are for sale. Cheap. The village of two thousand is a gumbo of Cajun crawfishermen, Vietnamese shrimpers, black and white catfish plant workers, and a few passing-through tourists drawn to the levee's boat landings by interstate billboards advertising swamp tours. The town's main industry is crawfish, catfish, and seafood processing. More than two dozen businesses deal with crawfishing in the Atchafalaya Basin either directly or indirectly. Most of the crawfish processing plants employ women as peelers, and during the season buses bring more from Mexico to swell the work force.

There is an Hebert (pronounced *A-bear*) supermarket in town, as well as one of the ubiquitous Dollar General stores that have invaded the South. And there is T-Sue's Bakery—outside, a sign wih a red light proclaims, "Hot French Bread When Flashing."

Other towns in the area—dubbed Acadiana by legislative decree—have beautiful, poetic, French-y names. There's lovely little Breaux Bridge, only six miles away, and St. Martinville, also called Le Petit Paris, and the musical-sounding Catahoula and Cecilia, all in the same St. Martin Parish. And the big city nearby is Lafayette, a university town with oil millionaires and gorgeous churches and endless modern subdivisions. After the twin terrors of Hurricanes Katrina and Rita, the population of Lafayette grew to more than two hundred thousand.

Then, last and least, there's unromantic-sounding Henderson. Plain old Henderson.

WE PAID LITTLE ATTENTION to Henderson or its uninspired name that first day, hardly noticing it, driving straight through what passes for the main business district—a small hardware store, a drugstore, Amy's grocery, and a couple of popular Cajun restaurants—across a bridge to the levee.

The levee is its own world. Two roads run parallel—a dirt one atop the levee and a paved one beside it. Every now and then the two roads are conjoined by a gravel exit, which lets you crawl up the dirt mound from the pavement and across the dirt levee. Suddenly, at the top, you get an elevated view of Henderson Lake and the Atchafalaya swamp. It is breathtakingly beautiful, no matter how many times you've seen it, a picture postcard of cypress trees and stumps and snowy egrets that fill the trees like Christmas ornaments.

That first day, window-shopping the swamp, we topped the levee and parked our car at a sweet little bait shop beneath a sign that said Basin Landing Marina. It looked for all the world like the set of that old movie, *Tammy and the Bachelor*, with an innocent Debbie Reynolds in the title role and living on her grandfather's houseboat in the swamp. We got out to nose around. Houseboats of every size and description stretched for about a quarter mile along the shoreline. Some of the boats were real fancy yachts, sea-going size. Others were more like floating single-wide trailers, homemade rigs with fanciful names. Most were stamped with the personality of their owners and of the swamp. There were swinging squirrel tails on the porches, or last year's Christmas lights still strung.

The houseboat tied closest to the marina store was also the smallest at the landing, a one-room affair with a deep front porch. Its exterior was wrapped in pale lime vinyl, with pieces of the faux wood coming loose, and there was an interesting piece of driftwood crowning the door. The boat had a tin top and an exposed, outdoor hot water heater. The decking was painted a darker green, and there were metal eyelets where a porch swing once had hung. It looked a lot like the playhouse I'd had as a child, which remains the most exciting bit of real estate I've ever owned. The houseboat was, in all ways, to both of us, the most appealing boat at the landing. Its name was printed across the front: *The Green Queen.* Of course. Nailed to the front window was another sign: For Sale.

We stood there staring, not speaking, each knowing instinctively that the other was not going to behave sensibly this time, or attempt to stop his mate from acting impulsively. We both wanted that little houseboat, moored as it was so far from our jobs, our home, and our lives.

"You need dat boat, you."

A jolly, rotund man had appeared from nowhere, looking part used-car salesman, part ancient mariner. His hair was combed back like a mature Elvis, and he wore blousy knit pants that had elastic at their ankles and zebra stripes all over. He spoke with a heavy Cajun accent, that remarkable patois of archaic French sprinkled with American English.

"Get down and come see," he invited.

We'd soon learn that "get down" is Cajun for "get out and come in," as in "get out of the car and come into the house."

We got down.

The smooth salesman's name was Johnelle Latiolais; he and his beautiful wife, Jeanette, ran the marina then. We didn't know it yet, of course, but Johnelle loves and understands people. He loves people even more than he loves wheeling and dealing. He had, in a previous professional life, been a car salesman. He is smart and can be relentless. He certainly recognized two easy marks from out-of-town when he saw them. We were all but salivating.

Johnelle miraculously found the front door key to the *Green Queen* in his pants pocket and gave us the short tour of its one room. There was a set of bunk beds, a sofa bed, a kitchen sink, and a propane-fueled stove top. The inside was freshly painted. The old boat had seen better days, but inside it was dry and cozy. It floated on a small barge and old plastic oil drums. Soon enough, but in his own time, Johnelle revealed the low, low price. This was one heckuva deal, he insisted, and the boat probably would be sold before day's end; if not today, certainly tomorrow.

Months later, after we knew him much better, Johnelle would say we'd paid at least a couple of thousand dollars too much for the *Queen*. He was aggravatingly, belatedly honest that way, telling you what you should have done only when it was too late to correct your mistake. He knew the details of every financial transaction that happened in town, and he regularly was a party to many of them.

Don asked Johnelle about the duck hunting prospects on Henderson Lake, the part of the swamp we were looking out at from the *Green Queen*'s little dock. Johnelle, comfortable in his high-salesman mode, rhapsodized about the endless duck bounty, the spectacular fishing, the incomparable fun it was to spend all your weekends and family holidays at the lively landing. Why, he much preferred living at the marina to living at his real home. So did Jeanette, he added.

After we knew him better, Johnelle would say how much

he'd missed being at his own home while running the marina. And Jeanette, it turned out, was a passionately dedicated mother and grandmother who loved home more than anyone I've ever known. She almost had been tortured by living so far—the two miles—from her real home during their marina career.

But Johnelle was on a mission. He was the Old Man and we were the big fish. We took his business card.

By the time we made the long drive home to Atlanta, back to our rather white bread, everyday lives, we had convinced one another that we absolutely needed a houseboat on the Atchafalaya Swamp. At the time I was struggling with a four-columns-a-week job at *The Atlanta Journal-Constitution*; Don still commuted to Birmingham and taught a full load of classes at UAB. We lived in the Atlanta suburb of Carrollton, Georgia, and additionally kept up, as best we could, my money pit of an old farmhouse in north Mississippi. Not to mention Don had an old trailer on Smith Lake near Birmingham where he loved to spend time with his brother. We were property poor and over-extended. We knew we would, in reality, have precious little time to be bobbing on Henderson Lake in a shanty boat called the *Green Queen*.

That, of course, didn't stop us. Our other residences and responsibilities weren't even speed bumps. Don saw the *Green Queen* as an ideal hunting camp, a place to spend his Thanksgiving to New Year's vacation from classes. I saw it as a refuge from deadlines and editors' phone calls and, frankly, reality. The whole swampy area had an exotic, foreign, surreal feel, and yet you didn't need a long plane ride or a passport to reach the place. It was, we thought, the best solution for two working stiffs, die-hard Southerners who also are incurable Francophiles.

As soon as we got home, Don phoned the number on Johnelle's card. We'd be sending a check. That very day. Please don't sell our boat.

Johnelle, on the other end of the line, congratulated us on our sound personal decision and shrewd business deal. I'm pretty positive that when he hung up the phone Johnelle and Frank and Dan and the other denizens of Basin Landing had, at our expense, one of those brisk, laughter-filled conversations in French that we soon would be hearing often. Johnelle had hooked the city slickers with one worm and landed a tidy commission. We hadn't even dickered over his asking price.

I immediately started thinking of even quasi-legitimate stories with a Louisiana angle and marking the calendar to see when we'd next get to visit Henderson. Once I put my mind to it, there seemed a million Louisiana stories that Atlantans might enjoy reading.

At the time, I thought we might keep the *Queen* for a duck season or two. Funny, we said, how a bogus boar hunt had ended up in this bizarre purchase.

We had no way of knowing that this boat deal would change and thereby enrich our lives, giving them a cultural dimension few are privileged to enjoy. Though never to be natives, we would become more than guests. Henderson would be our second home, our holiday and winter destination of choice, for the next decade.

And that charming Cajun Falstaff, fixer, bon vivant, and salesman extraordinaire, Johnelle, along with his long-suffering and sweet wife Jeanette, soon would become our new best friends.

Fried Turkey, Stewed Cajuns

Spending Thanksgiving holiday on the *Green Queen* was my idea. I imagined cool, lovely nights on the house-boat, listening to swamp sounds, enjoying a respite from the city and deadlines. I planned my wardrobe—jeans and overalls—and packed only the essentials: good music and bug repellent.

Don took no persuading. It was duck season. He couldn't wait to roar away into predawn darkness in his little skiff, and quickly began studying maps of the lake and all its cypress obstacles. He was more than ready.

We arrived in the swamp around midnight in midweek. The marina at Basin Landing was just as I had imagined—lonely, dead silent, an owl perched atop a vapor lamp looking for wayward critters in the pool of spotlight below. We quietly unloaded our gear and marveled anew at how compact and yet complete the houseboat was. Why everything a person needed was right here, in one room.

We slept like babies on the *Queen* that night, her jalousie windows open to catch the fall breeze. I probably dreamed of floating in a pirogue through purple water hyacinths. I'm relatively sure Don dreamed of killing the limit.

The ruckus began before sunlight the next morning. There

was the righteous roar of outboard motors, dozens of them, some right outside our window. There was the clinking and clanking of trailers as fishermen and hunters launched their boats. There were pounding footsteps on the labyrinth of wooden ramps that—in a design by Rube Goldberg—connected the docks one to the other. The night before the place had appeared empty, but suddenly it was the Grand Central Station of the swamp.

The noise never abated. As the hunters returned that morning at what seemed like five-minute intervals, the raucous parties began. People were shouting greetings to one another and playing lively French tunes on radios. Something that smelled good was cooking on every boat, at every camp. The short walk from the *Queen* to the marina office was like a stroll through a long buffet line. And at the office, Johnelle and Jeanette were whupping up a gumbo. Whenever you had business at the office, Johnelle would lift the pot lid and let you sample.

It was easy to make friends at Basin Landing. There's been a lot written and said about the "shy people" of Bayou Country—there's even a movie about the area by that name—and some of that is true. Until they know you, and what you want, the Cajun people are, as a sensible rule, reluctant to chat.

Part of the reason for that apparent shyness, at least with the older people, stems from their not knowing English very well. Many in the over-seventy crowd speak only Cajun French. It is their first language. When you enter the M&M bait shop on the main road in Henderson, for example, a table full of old men will be swapping fish stories in French. Johnelle and Jeanette, though fluent in English, speak Cajun French to one another whenever it's just the two of them.

That said, once a Cajun does get to know you and trusts you, he'll tell you his life story in three minutes. He will also ask how much you paid for the watch on your arm, why you would live anywhere but in Louisiana, and how many miles are on your vehicle. It's the opposite of live and let live; it's more like mind my business, and I'll mind yours.

One of our first good friends was Frank, a handsome, fortyish marina employee who could have been a cover boy for any outdoors magazine. He had a winning personality as well. Everyone loved Frank. He was funny, swamp-savvy, and loved telling stories about himself in the third person.

They make a lot of movies in the picturesque swamp. There have been Penthouse shoots and Hallmark Hall of Fame movies filmed right in Henderson Lake. Robert Duvall's wonderful indie film, *The Apostle*, used our swamp as a backdrop.

One day, when Hollywood was busy staging a scene near the marina, Frank was cutting the grass. The production company sent someone over to ask Frank to cut off his noisy mower for the duration of the shoot.

"The man doesn't pay Frank *not* to cut the grass," the unflappable Frank told the Hollywood envoy. "The man pays Frank to cut the grass."

The movie person handed Frank a hundred dollar bill. Frank killed the mower.

At this point in his story Frank, who told it more than once, would pause dramatically, look toward the heavens, and then say in a triumphant roar: "Frank felt a drunk front moving in!"

Normally, you didn't have to bribe Frank to find him obliging. He was, in fact, a genie of sorts. Unless you rubbed him the wrong way, he was at your disposal. If you even mentioned you might like to try something—a duck hunt in a remote part of the lake, a ride on an airboat—he'd deliver your wish to you on a silver platter.

Frank had an amazing creative streak. His duck blind was

the best in the swamp, a contraption that used hollow cypress stumps to hide the hunter, and looked like a bit of free-floating Atchafalaya. A thing of beauty, really, as creative a disguise as a Mardi Gras mask.

I casually asked Frank one day about fried turkey. Was it any good? Though it had become quite popular all over, I'd never tried it. Frank insisted that he'd fry a turkey for us, at the *Queen*, on Thanksgiving Day.

Thanksgiving, of course, is celebrated with family in Cajun Country, same as elsewhere. Cajuns are even more family oriented than most Americans. It is not unusual for Cajun children to live within a stone's throw of their parents, who live just as close to the grandparents. Sometimes the Henderson yards full of generations of houses remind me of diagramming sentences in school, with the children and grandchildren as modifiers of the root words. NFL football star Jake Delhomme, worth millions, built his big house within a literal stone's throw of his parents' residence, just off a busy highway between his hometown of Breaux Bridge and Lafayette. He first refurbished his grandfather's house, which now sits in his backyard.

Frank, however, was nobody's idea of a perfect family man. He was enduring a bitter separation and was estranged from his wife and children. In late-night bull sessions on the *Green Queen*, he already had told us more than we wanted to hear about the situation, which involved brawls and bills and ultimately another woman. We weren't all that surprised he was free to spend Thanksgiving at the marina, with us.

Still, I wanted the day to be special for everyone. With typical and unnecessary fussiness, I rushed to the nearest dollar store and bought four real plates; the plastic ones on the *Queen* simply wouldn't do for a holiday meal with visitors. I also bought table linens, which really might have been overkill considering there wasn't a table. I bought fresh flowers for a centerpiece.

Frank and his new girlfriend arrived early in the morning in Frank's ancient blue pickup full of dents. Frank had a story that went with each dent. His friend was a former exotic dancer, the mother of five children, grandmother of several, and carried around with her what seemed a Rolodex of miseries. While I deviled eggs, she drank a beer and shared a life's story that would have embarrassed Jerry Springer. There were divorces, dead husbands, lost children, and lawsuits. The child welfare people figured into her sordid tale at regular intervals. And I couldn't help but notice both Frank and his sweetheart were pretty well into their cups before the cooking even started.

Frank, when sober, was an excellent cook. Even Jeanette, who may be the best cook in a parish known for good cooks, often complimented Frank on his culinary talents. Turns out he was a pretty good cook when drunk, too. He set to work on the turkey, injecting it with seasoning, heating oil to just the right temperature and finally dropping the bird into the hot grease.

The smell was heavenly. Our little dock had become a gourmet deli. I made too many side dishes, put the flowers into a vase and set appetizers in reach of the cook and his girl. They were not tempted.

While the turkey fried, Frank and the dancer drank beer. And drank some more. They didn't touch the appetizers, or even mention how good the turkey was smelling. They avoided food like I avoid snakes. By about one, the bird was done.

I set a borrowed table—Jeanette and Johnelle were a never-ending source for whatever we needed—with my four new plates on the porch of the *Green Queen*. The day was warm and pleasant and, for once, the marina was perfectly quiet.

The other boats' owners were home with their families for the holiday. The lake was an azure oasis behind us. The layout would have looked swell on a magazine cover. Frank delivered the perfectly cooked turkey to a big platter, and I suggested the obvious, that we all sit down and eat.

"You eat," he said. "We'll eat later."

Nothing we could say could convince Frank or his partner to even taste the bird he'd spent the whole morning cooking. They sat off to the side of the porch, drinking beer, watching us eat.

I have never endured a Thanksgiving meal so awkward, yet at the same time so delicious. The two empty place settings reminded us to make conversation now and again, best we could, with our drinking visitors. There was ten times as much food as two people needed, of course.

We would understand in time—this Thanksgiving being our first lesson—that this day's behavior perfectly fit Frank's drinking pattern. Once he started drinking, he didn't like to eat and end the buzz. He would cook all night or all day for friends and then refuse to touch what he'd prepared so he could make the most of his drinking. This technique landed him in ditches, divorce court, and more than once, jail.

Frank, in fact, was a trusty working in the kitchen of the St. Martin parish jail when Cuban prisoners took it over, held the sheriff prisoner and made their demands on TV for better treatment. The incident made national news. Frank was proud of his eyewitness status and told funny stories about it from bar stools once he was released.

Henderson is not a place that frowns on drinking. As is the case in most of south Louisiana, you can buy liquor at the grocery store and the drugstore any day of the week. We emerged once from the *Green Queen* to find a leaflet tucked under the windshield wiper of our truck. "Courville Benefit Dance," it read:

> Mr. Daniel Courville recently died of cancer, leaving his wife Jane, who is also a cancer victim, in financial need. For years, Daniel and Jane were regulars at Whiskey River every Sunday. Daniel was known to people as the man who danced with the can of beer on his head . . . A benefit dance is being organized by friends and relatives in order to aid Jane . . ."

Yet even in this context, in a region wide open and wicked and known for its alcohol consumption, Frank, friends said, drank far too much. And when he drank, he wasn't his sweet, funny self. He forgot about work, or money he owed, not to mention his manners. Sadly, not long after our memorable and deep-fat-fried Thanksgiving, Frank left the marina, his job, Henderson, and his family. Last I heard, Frank and the dancer and several of her children and their children were living in a crowded trailer in Breaux Bridge. We didn't see him much after our first year in the swamp. He told Don, who inquired about it, that he no longer had any interest in duck hunting. All of us missed him, and we never had fried turkey for Thanksgiving again.

Catahoula Cajun
Truck-Driving Mama

A poboy is a sandwich built on French bread like the biblical house on a firm foundation. A pile of fried shrimp on a hamburger bun, or on any other kind of bread, is just a sandwich. A poboy on French bread takes that same shrimp to another, higher, celestial level.

I have often pondered what I might want to eat if I were convicted of a serious crime, sentenced to die, and allowed one last meal. I vacillate between a fried oyster poboy and a fried shrimp poboy, depending on the season, my mood, and a few other hot grease variables.

Poboy joints are everywhere in south Louisiana. They are as ubiquitous as the drive-through daiquiri stands that amaze and amuse outlanders. The drive-through daiquiri in Henderson is named The Smoker Friendly, about as politically incorrect an institution as you could conjure. It does a smoking business. There is an open-container law in Louisiana; that is, you are by law prohibited from having open alcoholic beverages in either the driver's or passenger seats. Still, the drive-through joints thrive and no posse waits for you at the exit, one of the many ironies of Louisiana law.

One March day Don and I were standing in line at our

next-to-favorite poboy restaurant, Chicken on the Bayou. Our absolute, number one favorite is Bon Creole in New Iberia, a cinderblock joint with a windowless exterior. Joe and Jean Barlow, two of my more cautious Iuka, Mississippi, friends, took one look at the place and refused to go inside. They are used to more upscale restaurants. Once their organdy sensibilities got past the Bon Creole's humble looks, they loved its food.

At the Chicken on the Bayou, the runner-up in our perennial poboy rankings, I've ordered and eaten everything on the menu—shrimp, crawfish, oysters, boudin balls, red beans and rice—everything but its namesake chicken. Chicken on the Bayou [see also page 113] is mostly a take-out restaurant, which also sells lewd postcards of alligators nipping at bare female buttocks, alligator-toe keychains and Honorary Coonass bumperstickers. Chicken on the Bayou makes Bon Creole look like the Ritz.

We were waiting in line to order crawfish poboys, our customary March order because in March the crawfish season is wide open and the crawfish is fresh. The proprietor was playing a tape, a lively country album sung in French. That's not unusual in south Louisiana, to turn on the radio and hear country standards you've heard all of your life, only sung in French. Talk about the best of all possible worlds. Hillbilly singing in French.

The woman singing on the tape this day sounded just like Kitty Wells, only on key, which Kitty wasn't always, and in French.

"Who is that?" Don asked the owner, pointing to the ceiling the way you do when you are asking about heavenly music.

The owner said it was Hélène Boudreaux from over in Breaux Bridge.

WE DECIDED THEN AND there we had to find Hélène Boudreaux, which turned out to be easy. Information had her phone number. I set up an interview right away and wrote about her for the Atlanta newspaper. CNN followed up with a feature story, which delighted the swamp chanteuse. We soon became good friends.

Hélène bills herself as the "Catahoula Cajun Truck-Driving Mama," not as snappy a sobriquet as, say, "The Possum," but an effectively succinct and apt bio. Hélène grew up the daughter of French-speaking sharecroppers in Catahoula, a pretty little town about ten miles south of Henderson on the very edge of the Atchafalaya. As a child she picked cotton and peppers to help dirt-poor parents feed their eight sons and six daughters. Hélène married too young and too often and raised up her own eight babies as best she could. And she passionately loved music.

One day, after all her children were grown, she found another passion, one that paid. One of her exes had been a trucker, a good one, and had taught her all he knew about the big rigs. She decided to try the lonesome life herself.

"My sweet Cajun music will not put food on my table," Hélène remembers thinking as she drove north from home. "I remember crying like a baby each time I lost another Cajun radio station . . ."

It turned out that she enjoyed the freedom of the road. Missed the sugarcane fields and the sweet night sounds of the swamp, but found the hard-traveling life exciting. She won safety awards and even became an instructor for one company that hired her. Her bright blue Peterbilt had pink, ladylike appointments. She drove eighteen wheelers for a decade before she hurt her back. It nearly killed her to give it up. But that's when she returned to her first love, music.

At age fifty-four, Hélène bought a used guitar and rented a library video to teach herself to play it. The singing she knew how to do. She'd been singing, flat out, since she was a little girl working in the sugarcane fields. She sang as a struggling young mother. And she sang while she criss-crossed the country with long hauls in her semi.

"I'd sing on my CB whenever I'd drive through Nashville. That way I could say I'd been on the air in Nashville," she said.

No hillbilly singer ever found more honest material to work with than Hélène, who writes her own songs and also sings country standards—often in French. For song-writing grist, she has bad men, long hauls, short marriages, and hard times. She knew shotgun houses and hand-me-down clothes. Compared to Hélène, Tammy Wynette slept on a bed of American Beauties and Loretta Lynn grew up wealthy.

Today Hélène lives in an old red house with a wide screened porch that sits close by a canal with a musical name: Butte La Rose. The woods all around are carpeted with fern, and at night you hear a steady chorus of tree frogs. The holiday camps strung like a Mardi Gras parade from Hélène's place to the nearby Atchafalaya River have whimsical names: Deep Purple, Dad's Pad When Mom's Mad, The Black Pot. Hélène's place is called Camp Catahoula, after her hometown.

Hélène seems completely at peace here, one with sweet swamp fragrances and natural sounds. A striking redhead, Hélène serves as a voluptuous figurehead for that long parade of funky camps, an exotic yet natural woman, from her green thumbs to her flowing skirts.

The little red house itself is a story. Hélène was living in a trailer in Breaux Bridge. But she owned the Butte La Rose land and had heard about a house–or camp, as the Cajuns invariably call their holiday homes—for sale to be moved. The owner was asking $6,000. Hélène offered him $1,000. He countered with $5,000. Hélène offered $1,000 again. Sensing the uselessness of such haggling, he told her, "Just take it." And she did, giving rooms-to-go a whole new meaning.

The wrap-around screen porch is now a small forest, full of Hélène's potted plants and cages for her mourning doves. I think it may be one of the best porches in America, at least one of the most complete, with a spare chifferobe and cast iron cookware, places to sit and that bounty of potted green. Outside she has blue bottles dangling from a cypress tree, the proverbial bottle tree to keep the evil spirits away.

HÉLÈNE SINGS AND PERFORMS regionally, and has even been recognized by the acclaimed Cajun French Music Association, which honors the area's most talented musicians. Twice she's won the "Female Vocalist of the Year" category of the Cajun French Music Awards, plus the CFMA's Heritage Award for her work with young musicians. Many of the young Cajuns you see on Leno or Letterman—the amazing little blond accordion player Hunter Hayes comes to mind—have played with Hélène beneath the trees outside a Breaux Bridge restaurant called Bayou Boudin. She went on a mission to keep the music alive by encouraging the young and the willing. One of her countless musical projects was an album of nigh-forgotten French ballads, *Chanson d'Avant Les Bals*, sung a cappella. When you hear those haunting tunes sung by Hélène, you know the meaning of perfect pitch. She sings at funerals, weddings, in restaurants and bars. She sings wherever there's a gathering that needs music to make it better. She sings when all alone.

A lot of what's left of her time is spent generously recognizing other musicians, herding them into informal ceremonies—

or catching them on the fly—and presenting them with her handmade certificates. Tangible and rare gratitude, suitable for framing. She feels strongly that one way to preserve the remarkable culture is to honor the musicians who have kept it alive.

Hélène wrote and self-published a book, *Cajun Survivor,* several pounds of loosely edited autobiography that detail her failed marriages and truck-driving misadventures and the struggles of raising a passel of children alone. She also writes a newsy, sometimes poetic column about goings-on in Butte La Rose for the weekly *Teche News.* If that's not enough, Hélène also is a traiteur, Cajun for a traditional healer who prays over maladies from chicken pox to cancer. In Paris, "le traiteur" is a caterer, but in Henderson "traiteur" means healer. And there's a lot to be healed in Henderson.

A friend of ours, Ann Morell, was visiting from Mississippi, and one day I drove her out to Hélène's. Hélène's house is quite often a stop on my informal tours of the countryside when friends visit. For one thing, the location is beautiful. And, if my timing is lucky, Hélène just might be sitting outside on the wide porch steps and in the mood to sing. It never takes much arm-twisting to have Hélène burst into song, rendering, in perfect pitch, the song she wrote about her hometown, "Ma Belle Catahoula," or any other request a tourist might make. It's an experience visitors never forget. Once or twice I've presumed to drive up with friends before Hélène was dressed and receiving; Hélène is not immune to vanity, and likes to look presentable before she performs, even informally. She politely told me, "Another time."

This particular day, when Ann was with me, Hélène welcomed us with open arms, the way she usually does. My older friend was suffering with a nerve problem in her shoulder.

Ann apologized for her bent posture and explained what was causing it.

"I could pray on that," Hélène said, and Ann quickly accepted.

Next thing I knew, Hélène was sitting in the driver's seat of my van, one hand on Ann's problem shoulder. I couldn't hear the prayer, which I assumed was forthcoming, but the two of them seemed perfectly and instantly in sync, healer and patient.

Being a skeptic and heathen, I walked around outside to keep from jinxing the sure cure. I strolled through the Eden that is my favorite traiteur's yard while the two women, intent and oblivious, squeezed their eyes shut and rocked in unison inside the van. Watching from a safe distance, I wished for a moment that I could believe in such magic, could believe that prayers from a certain someone had weight with the Powers that Be, if, indeed, there be any. It would be downright convenient to have in your stable of friends a generous woman who could, through divine contacts, banish a wart, or cure a cancer.

I'm afraid I believe most profoundly in Hélène's extraordinary musical gift. I believe her voice could move mountains and tame lions. She has an angel's tonsils. There are no doubting Thomases when it comes to her voice. Even some of my stuffier musician friends who don't care for Cajun or Country admit that Hélène is incredible. She carries around with her a black book the size of the Manhattan phone directory. In it are the words to hundreds of songs, a collection she began years ago and that keeps growing. As long as she has an audience—of any size—Hélène will sing her heart out. If you invite her to supper, she brings her guitar. You don't have to ask or wheedle. She will sing for an audience of one or a thousand and with the same intensity and enthusiasm. She can even yodel.

Since childhood Hélène has idolized most country music stars, especially Merle Haggard and some of the other more traditional singers. When she got the chance to sing a warm-up performance for the legendary Ray Price at an old Alabama theater, Hélène was beside herself with excitement. She planned on singing some of Price's signature songs, only in French. She rehearsed and rehearsed.

The night of the Ray Price concert Hélène arrived early. She looked beautiful, and exotic, the way some Cajuns do when out of context. In her purple sweater and swirling skirt and dangling earrings, she was like a tropical bird loose from its cage. Ray Price, on the other hand, arrived late. His entourage had taken a wrong turn, and he was irritable and, I dare to say, not in particularly good voice. Hélène was on stage and singing before Price made it to the auditorium. He finally walked into the wings to listen.

"Who is that woman, and why is she stealing all my material?" he asked no one in particular. Price wasn't joking, either. He spoke with rancor. Hélène finished her performance and rushed to meet him. She hadn't heard him grouse about her act. Hélène gushed over the star and asked him to pose with her for a snapshot. He grudgingly obliged.

Unlike Hélène, I have never been a huge Ray Price fan; his sound is far too smooth and his accompaniment overly orchestrated for the country genre. I'm more of a roots music kind of gal, preferring the industrial-strength, tears-in-your-beer, traditional approach.

After that night, I wouldn't cross the street to hear Ray Price sing. Price, far as I know, never wrote a song. He made a fabulous living singing the songs of others. When he first got started, he aped Hank Williams, once his Nashville roommate. Price evidently changed that shtick when he had to admit to himself there were too many Hank wannabes on the market.

But, then, Willie Nelson likes Ray Price, so he must not be all bad.

Hélène got into the game late. Ain't it funny how time slips away? Living her extraordinary life gave her plenty to sing and write about, but she's had to put the pedal to the metal to get it done. Less time but more material. If only fate had let her skip a few jumps, pass Go, and collect two hundred dollars. I can see a young, red-headed Hélène on the stage of the Grand Ole Opry, rich and famous and married to her manager, living in a garish Nashville mansion with music notes on the gate and money to burn. If only there were creative justice, not just the poetic kind. Talent and luck don't always ride tandem. Any honest person would know and admit that.

Big Ears and Alligators

J
ohnelle and the boys at the landing call Doug Mequet "Big Ears." Everyone in Cajun Country wears a colorful nickname, partly because the surnames are so few. The Henderson/Breaux Bridge phone book is the only one in the country that I know of to use nicknames in its listings, necessary to avoid confusion. That way, amongst the countless Thibodeauxs, Boudreauxs, Latiolaises, Mequets, and Guidrys, you can find the person you want to call.

"In 1949, the local operator was replaced with a dial system and the publication of the first local telephone directory," the phone book says. "The directory was confusing because of the duplication of names and many people didn't know what their neighbors' given names were . . ."

Not everyone has his nickname published, but hundreds request it. That way, if you are trying to ring up Kojack Thibodeaux you won't get Coot Thibodeaux instead. Or Toie Guidry when you actually wanted Stretch.

Not long after buying the *Queen*, we made the acquaintance of a Bugsy, a Big Daddy, a Bubby. There also was a Half-Pint, two men called Happy, and carpenter brothers Dado and Darling. Half-Pint was a colorful swamp guide and photographer and the author of a children's book about his dog; Half-Pint died a few years ago. Dado Latiolais had a major speaking role in the wonderful Hallmark Hall of Fame movie, *Old Man*, based on a Faulkner short story and filmed in Atchafalaya Swamp.

The point is, we knew them all by their nicknames. The women usually are spared. Incidentally, the female Cajun names are more often French than those of the males. We know, for instance, several Jeannettes and Emmelines, but no Pierres.

A Cajun waitress is more likely to call a customer "Boo" than "Honey." "Boo" and "Cher" are catch-all endearments, and "Cher" can even be used between two males to mean "buddy" or "pal." You see a lot of names that begin with either "Tee" or simply "T," as in T-Bob, T-Don, T-Sue. The "T" or "Tee" is short for "petit," French for little, of course. The "T" takes the place of "junior" when a son is named for his father. So, you have Little Bob, et cetera.

The first day Johnelle called me Boo I felt proud. Never mind he uses it for babies, old ladies, the occasional dog, and total strangers. It felt like acceptance to me. Who wants to be the only person in town without a colorful nickname? Don visits the M&M Sporting Center for coffee after hunting ducks. The folks there have nicknamed him One Duck Don. They jokingly accuse him of waving one old stuffed duck each morning as a sign of fresh accomplishment.

Nicknames are more than a straight road to identification here. They also are a free and creative way of having fun, and the Cajuns are masters of that. It is one thing I quickly grew to admire about the culture. There's a capacity for merry-making that seems bottomless. In the Mississippi Delta the poor sing the blues; in Cajun Louisiana the poor tell an elaborate joke. Over the years they edit, refine, and perfect the same joke. A funny story, no matter how many times it is told, no matter how many times you may hear it, remains funny. It, in fact, grows funnier with each telling. A Cajun story ages well. Like fine wine, or Normandy cheese. It is not unusual to hear the punch line of a joke that was successful in the morning repeated all day long.

A funny nickname basically works the same way. Whenever Mr. Doug walks into a room and Johnelle hollers out, perhaps for the millionth time, "Hey, Big Ears!" the room rocks with laughter. In Henderson it would be rude *not* to laugh at one grown man calling another "Big Ears."

Johnelle's jokes are almost never politically correct and probably would not find favor over at the university in Lafayette, fifteen miles and a world away. Fat women he calls "Wide Load." Sometimes to their face. Everyone in Henderson calls one another, not to mention themselves, "coonass." I cannot imagine a full conversation with any of our Henderson friends without the word in play. The use of "coonass" sparks a perennial debate on the pages of the Lafayette newspaper and elsewhere, with Cajun folks divided about its humor and appropriateness. The origin remains a complete mystery, though there are several theories, each more out of left field than the last. Lafayette, as mentioned, is a university town and its Cajun residents are more than a little self-conscious about their identities.

The rest of the area seems to feel differently. A straw poll by the New Iberia newspaper once found that sixty percent of its readership opposed legislative condemnation of the word "coonass"—after a political crusade to do just that. In 1974 the Louisiana legislature finally condemned the word by resolution, calling it "offensive, vulgar, and obscene." But the fancy-pants resolution means little to most working-class Cajuns, many of whom regard the label as a badge of ethnic pride. No less than Ronald Reagan, campaigning in Louisiana in 1976, called himself an "honorary Cajun coonass." Johnelle, staring at a photograph of himself in a snowfall in north Mississippi, declared philosophically, typically: "That's one frozen coonass."

Former Louisiana State University football coach Nick Saban most recently angered some by his off-the-record use of the word "coonass." But then, most of Louisiana already was angry with Saban because he'd left LSU, taken a professional football coaching job—bad enough—then soon left the pros to coach at LSU's Southeastern Conference rival, the University of Alabama. The ensuing debate over his use of the word was the same as always; some said it was a slur, others thought not.

Even the term "Cajun," slang for the more formal *Acadian*, was at first not accepted easily by the more activist or elitist groups who, understandably, fought anything that threatened to kill culture by assimilation.

Coonass aside, nicknames are almost obligatory in the Cajun culture. Johnelle usually calls Don "Boudreaux," as in the popular, endless Boudreaux and Thibodeaux jokes about two witless Cajun men, the Amos and Andy of the swamp. One day the two of them—Johnelle and Don, a.k.a. Boudreaux and Thibodeaux—were buying shrimp from a woman running a wayside seafood stand by a busy road in Lafayette.

"You better get more than ten pounds, Boudreaux," Johnelle advised Don. Johnelle is always free and insistent with advice. "I'm telling you, Boudreaux. You're feeding a lot of people, you."

When Don *Grierson* handed over his credit card, the woman looked at it and back at Don, her face full of a twice-bitten merchant's suspicion. "I thought you were a Boudreaux," she said, eyeing Don. Johnelle, of course, collapsed with laughter. The rest of the week he'd say, "I thought you were a Boudreaux" and laugh and laugh.

There's an auto repair shop in town called Moss', for the owner, a man everyone calls Moss. I thought it was his last name. He explained that it's his nickname, a corruption of his first name, Thomas, which his father hollered out at dusk when it was time for his son to come in from playing. "Thom-MAS!" he would yell. And it sounded like "Moss." So that's what he became.

Not always is the inspiration for a nickname as obvious as with Big Ears. Sometimes there's even a sad irony. One of the two Happys—this one worked at the marina—killed himself not long after we bought the *Green Queen*. But, as with stereotypes, there's usually some kernel of truth behind the nickname. Doug's ears are huge, probably about six inches in length counting lobes. Adding a touch of irony is the fact he cannot hear it thunder. Doug worked on the offshore drilling platforms so long his big ears were rendered virtually useless.

Despite big ears, Doug Mequet is a handsome man, tall and white-haired with a booming voice and the heavy Cajun accent. He has had three wives, counting his present one, Emmeline. Doug's first two mates both died. The first, the mother of his sons, died tragically young of cancer. By all accounts, the big-hearted Doug faithfully nursed both of the women until the end. When we first met him, Doug was still working offshore and staying close to his second sick wife with her bad heart whenever he could be at home. He rarely left her side, unless she simply insisted that he take a break, which, to her credit, she quite often did. Whenever he found himself free for a rare day, Doug pulled his seldom-used pontoon boat to the landing, hooked up to electricity in the parking lot and camped out amongst the pickups and empty boat trailers. He rarely put the boat in the water; that might have made it too hard to get home to his wife had she needed him.

Doug typically spent his dry-dock camping day drinking beer and joking and talking around the potbelly stove in the marina store. This affable man was a favorite with the Basin

Landing denizens, even if they had to turn up the conversational volume several notches to accommodate him. In the evenings, he'd amble back to the pontoon and sleep. Doug, like everyone else in this blue-collar haven, went to bed early. People here— fishermen, hunters—are in perfect sync with the sun.

One cold winter's day, Doug came camping. Don, who keeps up with the weather anywhere we may be, is a virtual slave to the forecast in Henderson. Weather figures heavily into the movement of ducks, and ducks are Don's main business in Henderson. This day, with one ear to the radio, Don reported to me that a rare and bitter freeze was on its way. We cranked up the two electric heaters that kept the *Queen* toasty, bought steaks for supper, and settled in for a cozy evening.

Then I thought of Doug. I had seen him lumbering about the parking lot earlier, dressed in his usual coveralls, cold beer in one hand, big smile on his gentle face. Doug's disposition was always cheerful, never more so than when he was camping on his boat in the gravel parking lot.

"Let's invite Mr. Doug to dinner," I said. Don readily agreed. In other places, in Georgia or Mississippi where our other homes have been and are, Don's not much of a social animal. He figures he made all the friends he needed decades ago, and he doesn't suffer fools at all. In Henderson, everything changes. Henderson reminds Don of his hometown of Moss Point fifty years ago, he says, and so in Louisiana he's always ready for visitors, even fools. And in Louisiana, to entertain company, all you have to do is ask.

Doug arrived early and seemed to fill up the little house-boat with his huge presence. He bragged on my simple salad, the steak, the T-Sue Bakery bread. He's the kind of company that makes a cook feel really good, even when the cook is no cook. Cooking for Cajuns requires a certain temerity. They have a justified reputation for being good cooks; many Cajun men who served in World War II—if they weren't used on the front line as French interpreters—were valued as cooks. Don theorizes that Cajuns love their ubiquitous RVs because when they travel they can take their kitchens with them. Otherwise, a body could starve to death on the road.

Johnelle still complains about a hotdog he bought in Georgia thirty years ago. "There was no chili, no slaw, nuttin," he rails. "A bun and—splat!—a weenie. You call that a hotdog?"

I cooked for Doug on that frigid night, and he was appreciative. I think he wanted the company more than the food. He ate every morsel on his plate, then kicked back and told fascinating stories of supervising the offshore crews that bobbed about in the Gulf drilling for oil. I tried to ask questions at intervals, would have loved to have known the answers, but Doug never heard one word I hollered. He probably never will hear one word I say, I'm sincerely sad to report.

I've often thought Doug Mequet's family might be the perfect human illustration of what a typical, middle-class Cajun family looks like. After Louisiana oil was found in 1901, the sleepy agrarian life was changed forever. Swamps and bayous were polluted, but, on the positive side, men like Doug Mequet made good money and provided well for their families. If they survived the dangerous work on the rigs, they had pensions and nice retirements. The Mequets lived in a big brick house in Lafayette. Doug had two sons. One made a career of the military, the other worked long years for a sugarcane farmer before buying a houseboat marina on the levee. Oil, sugarcane, and the military are typical ways to make a living here. Henderson might be the area's biggest exception, where many still make their living in ways directly related to the swamp.

That cold night Doug stayed up pretty late, for him. He

eventually announced he was getting sleepy and needed to take his leave. He rose to walk the hundred yards to his boat, which, as usual, was parked on dry land.

"It's going to get mighty cold," Don said, announcing the obvious. "You do have a heater in there?"

"No," Doug said, patting his own ample middle, "but these coveralls are insulated. I'll be warm as toast."

Even on the *Green Queen*, two electric heaters blasting, it was a cold night. Outside the temperature dropped into the teens. It was the kind of bitter, damp, bone-numbing cold that it can be in Southern places on the water. I slept fitfully, thinking of poor Mr. Doug, nothing but padded coveralls to protect him from the frigid cold. I was pretty sure the next morning we'd find his big body in the pontoon, prone and frozen, big ears and all. *One frozen coonass.*

It might have been all the beer he drank, or the coveralls, or years of exposure to the elements offshore. That night Mr. Doug slept like a cypress log, full and inebriated and inert. He didn't really get cold, he said later, until he awoke, before dawn, as was his habit. Then he had a stout cup of coffee from Jeanette's pot with the rest of the early-bird Cajuns, talking and joking in French around the cozy stove. By the time I made it to the store, inquiring after poor Mr. Doug, he had pulled his campsite out of the parking lot and gone home to check on his sick wife.

DOUG WASN'T THE ONLY visitor on the houseboat, especially in warm weather. Once when we'd been away several months, Johnelle delighted in telling us an alligator had taken to sleeping on the *Queen's* back porch. Though it was often hard to tell when Johnelle was joking, this time he was dead serious.

Alligator sightings are common in the swamp, of course, and

tour guides know exactly where the gator holes are. Between tours, the savvy guides feed the gators to keep them in certain spots, the easier to amaze the tourists. Nothing thrills a touring group like a gator-sighting, unless it's the guide poking at the gator during the semi-dormant, cool days of spring.

I can handle the thought of an alligator using my porch when I'm not around. I'm not selfish. Besides, I never actually saw the transient gator, though I'm fully convinced it took advantage of our absences. Gators have that deceptive, slothful look, as if you could get a running start in a contest with one. In fact, they travel up to thirty miles an hour whenever the mood or need arises.

IT WAS THE SNAKES that gave, and give, me pause. When you've spent your childhood summers in south Georgia, where part of the daily routine involves slaying a rattlesnake, you grow a healthy respect for reptiles. How many days have I heard my grandfather calmly instruct us to get up on the porch, and then watch him disappear with a hoe. He'd return, the snake draped across the business end of the hoe like a flag of triumph, hollering out the all-clear. He kept the trophy rattles in his desk drawer, and we would dare one another to open it. Opening the drawer made a terrible, frightening, unmistakable racket. There's nothing that sounds remotely like it.

I hate snakes. All of them.

I remember reading once that the late writer Marjorie Kinnan Rawlings had the same fear and determined to conquer it. After all, she lived in a Florida swamp, that hammock called Cross Creek. She once took a hike with a snake in a knapsack on her back, tromping along with the knowledge a writhing creature was hitchhiking a ride. The behavioral exercise did not work. She remained scared of snakes, which were all too common at Cross Creek. Rawlings's biographer wrote that the writer used a copy of her first published book to beat to death a snake that had wandered into her cabin.

One March, we arrived at the *Green Queen* for a week's stay. It was a full ten degrees warmer in south Louisiana than it had been in Atlanta, and the snakes were stirring. Every time I opened the front door—the only door—to the *Queen*, a snake would be poking its head through the decking on the porch. Never mind that they were baby snakes, small and still a bit sluggish from the cool weather.

"Oh my God!" I'd scream, insisting Don escort me wherever I was going and use the paddle to kill or scare them, or both. I'd tap dance across the porch to the safety of the truck. I hate to be such a girl, and pride myself on always shouldering my load and being a true sport, but I do have limits.

Johnelle heard about my snake phobia and volunteered that the feed store over in Breaux Bridge had "Snake-Off," a chemical dust you sprinkle around an area that is supposed to keep snakes away. I never bought any, figuring the snakes simply would move in concentric circles, farther out, but still in my eventual path. Better to encounter and kill the beast when you first begin your journey.

Snakes remain the biggest obstacle between my desire and my ability to appreciate fully the great outdoors. I love to camp, hike, and canoe. Because of snakes, I usually wait until wintertime to indulge in those hobbies. I don't mind swatting mosquitoes or going without baths and makeup. That part of the deal is a true relief. I can shed a beauty regimen like those evil snakes do a skin. I dearly love leaving the telephone and television and computer behind. I'm about as low-tech as you can be and still hold a job in this century.

Snakes keep me from being a true outdoors adventurer.

I'm not proud of the fact, but it is one. I admire the way our friends here are nonchalant about snakes. Kelly, the youngest of Johnelle and Jeanette's two sons, doesn't use a gig when he goes out in the swamp at night after frogs. He simply sticks his hand in the snaky water and grabs the frogs. I know this because Don has gone with him and witnessed it.

I don't wish to be someone other than who I am, but I envy my Cajun friends their intimacy with nature. They have a healthy respect for snakes, but they don't let anything spoil the pure pleasure of outdoor life. I guess they weren't ordered to the porch whenever a snake entered the picture during their childhoods. They embrace whatever they pull into the pirogue with gusto and wonder, and can sleep in the cold and dark without trepidation. The line between the natural and manmade is blurred here, and that is a very good thing.

I find myself waiting from season to season to immerse myself in nature the way I know deep down that I could. In the fall, I fear getting shot by the ubiquitous deer hunters and decide, wisely I tell myself, to wait until winter to traipse through the woods. By winter, of course, the weather is cold and unpleasant and I decide to wait until spring when it makes a lot more sense to explore the Great Al Fresco. Spring works rather well until I see the first sluggish snake slithering from behind a rock, then I put my naturalist ambitions on a shelf until fall. Thus goes the vicious cycle.

One of these days I'm going to break these bonds of irrational fear and become one with the swamp and the snakes and the gators and whatnot. I'll go frog-gigging with Kelly and stick my bare hands into the dark water and pull a frog straight up to my mouth and kiss it. That act should cure me or kill me, give me warts or a prince, end my timid ways forever.

Hot French Bread
When Flashing

I was on my way to buy hot bread at T-Sue's Bakery when I saw a flier that announced the Henderson fire department would host a Christmas parade that very afternoon. I remembered the funky Crawfish Day parade I'd seen in Breaux Bridge one May at festival time; it included, among many other inexplicable and creative floats, Santa riding in a septic tank, though it was spring and the weather was balmy.

I decided to stay in town and wait for the parade. If May meant Santa tooling about in a septic tank, imagine what December might hold. I found a spot in the parking lot of a grocery called Amy's, pronounced *Ah-me* like a sweet sigh. Nothing is pronounced here like it looks. The restaurant nearest our house, Robin's, is not pronounced like the bird's name, for instance. It is *Row-ban*, similar to the sunglasses.

The parade was short, sweet, typical, I would learn after watching many future parades. There was the usual complement of beauty queens—Little Master Pincher (as in a crawfish pincher) and his tiny queen rode in a candy-apple-red convertible. Louisiana is as enthusiastic about beauty queens as Mississippi, and that's saying something. The Miss Smoked Meat crown illustrates the thoroughness of the system. As an old feminist, I've always had a problem with the beauty pageant culture. But the young Cajun women are so beautiful, typically with dark hair and eyes—most not Jolie Blondes at all until they find the dye pot. I suppose it would be a waste if they all turned up their noses at pageants, however anachronistic and sexist the events may be.

For this Henderson parade, my first, there also were noisy four-wheelers and go-carts and refurbished old cars and a few high-stepping horses. Many Cajuns love to ride horses, cowboy style, and have the perfect place to do so—on top of the levee. A lot of Cajuns are real cowboys, with cattle ranches still common in the prairies north and west of the swamp. It's not the image of the tourist brochures, where trappers and fishermen take center stage, but the cowpoke Cajun is a reality. The black Zydeco musicians have adopted the cowboy hat as part of their signature look, in fact.

The parade had little structure. Structure would be un-Cajun, or at least un-Henderson. Dignitaries, such as they were, threw candy to the children, but they also stopped and talked to friends along the route as the rest of the parade waited. What's your hurry? Good times don't roll on a schedule. Some in the parade threw beads left over from last year's Mardi Gras. Parades and festivals and decorations for every holiday are important here. When we bought the *Queen*—and for several years thereafter—the town of Henderson had no city sewage system, but it had lots of parties, parades, and a town Easter egg hunt. News of sewage system grants came and went, but not much seemed to be really happening on the solid waste front. Most residents had septic tanks in their yards. Others, and you could sniff out the difference, simply let their sewage pipes empty into ditches, creeks, or pastures. No sewage system, but a plethora of city-financed parades and street festivals each year. Celebrations are a high priority and always in the civic budget. The people of Henderson, despite limited resources, with or without civic underwriting, are darn good at celebrating.

DRIVING THE TWO MILES from T-Sue's to the levee at Christmastime is always a treat, with or without a parade. All the houses in town are bedecked with colored lights and gaudy tinsel, nothing white or demure, but dazzling, overwrought decorations the way you first loved them as a child. Anything that stays still long enough gets the treatment. A round propane tank is transformed into an orange snowman; it was painted orange for Halloween and served as a pumpkin. The artist just hasn't gotten around to repainting it white. Plastic milk jugs are filled with colored water. Reindeer prance across the metal roofs of double-wides. The nativity at Our Lady of Grace Catholic Church is positioned up off the ground on the wrought iron bell tower; it looks like a crèche prepared for high water, which, around here, may not be a bad idea.

For years I'd campaigned in my column against tasteful, tony, rich-people Christmas decorations; this little place required no such lectures. Henderson obviously prefers my kind of over-the-top, flat-out approach to decorating. There are plenty of mixed metaphors, Santas in helicopters hovering over Mary and the manger. There are homemade signs inviting Santa to stop, and starfish wreaths blinking. There are inflatable snow globes and reindeer and trees made out of lighted fishing nets. There are, as Rebecca Wells pointed out in her best-selling novels set in Louisiana, little altars everywhere, concrete statues of Mary that stay out year-round and get a hairnet of lights at Christmastime. There's one plywood silhouette of a soldier on his knees, his sub-machinegun beside him, kneeling at the cross. There's a reasonable facsimile of an ice rink with cheery, pink-cheeked cardboard skaters, none of them concerned about eighty-degree days melting their merriment.

After long years of observing decorating schemes all over the South, I feel safe in waxing axiomatic: The more money a person has, the less he spends on Christmas. I'm speaking universally here, or at least regionally, not about Henderson or Cajun Country. There are exceptions, but that's the general rule. At big houses where rich people live, you might see a single, subtle, live cedar wreath hanging on the wide front door. On a poor man's house the entire roof is covered with lights, which took half a day, a long ladder, and a great deal of courage to hang. Henderson, a town full of poor working people, has spectacular decorations.

Maybe poor people need the merriment more. Or maybe the rich got that way by scrimping on the important things in life like Christmas decorations. I'm not certain about that part.

Over the years, a lot of friends from other regions have visited us in Henderson, especially during the Christmas holidays. Either they come to duck hunt with Don, or to sample the food and music, or both. They appreciate the Christmas displays, or they don't. Nobody is ambivalent. Some are wise enough to keep quiet about their preferences. I take it personally when people prefer an Anglo-Saxon Christmas to the more garish French celebration. It's the difference between, say, a Maine Christmas and a Henderson one, or an Uptown versus Downtown.

I was in England once for what the British call "the run-up to Christmas." I saw the British approach to the holiday firsthand. The British employ their famous reserve even when it comes to decorating for Christmas. There is a sprig of holly here. A bit of cedar there. Fresh greenery is great, but it doesn't get a child's heart beating fast. It's for mature audiences only.

In England you don't see many Christmas lights at all. I walked by the Parliament building and was stunned. I've had bigger trees in my living room than they had on the grounds of their largest government institution. You wouldn't notice the British Parliament's tree if it were on Henderson's Main Street. It wouldn't compete.

The French, on the other hand, go for broke and probably go broke in the process. They opt for color and surplus. The results are spectacular. American snobs usually prefer the subtler approach. They use words like "tacky" and "too much." How can "too much" apply to Christmas?

But Henderson could have cared less what anyone else thought. This was a glorious, Cajun French Christmas. Even the flashing red light outside of T-Sue's seemed part of the display: Hot French Bread When Light Is Flashing. If the store is open, the light is flashing, like a beating heart, which would be appropriate; the bakeries in Cajun Country are the hearts of the towns.

AFTER THE PARADE, I rode around looking at all the lights. I felt inspired. Even vindicated. Finally, a place that subscribed to my over-the-top theory of decking the halls. Back at the *Queen*, I hung a green plastic wreath on the front door and, in the window, Budweiser frog lights I'd found for our boat in Mississippi's Bay St. Louis. Christmas in the swamp was as colorful as in town. The cypress trees had turned from green to red, and Henderson Lake was a brilliant blue under the winter sky. The swamp is an Eden in spring when the willows turn apple green. But I believe I love it most in December, when the boat traffic slows and the water is smooth as an egg and the marina is quiet.

Christmas morning dawned calm and private. Even the duck hunters took a break. The marina store was closed and we had the landing to ourselves. It was nice, but I wondered how Johnelle and Jeanette were spending the day and if they had made a gumbo. I wondered if Mr. Doug would show up on Christmas afternoon. If the truth be told, I felt a little left out. This wasn't our home. Not really. We didn't belong. We were glorified tourists. We didn't even speak the language. Maybe they were all laughing at us right now, around their respective Christmas trees, laughing at the silly duo who tries to assimilate during a few weeks' stay each year. Maybe we were being foolish.

We'd spent many happy days and nights on the *Green Queen*. We'd used it as the base for a second life—one free of deadlines. But the houseboats were strictly a vacation gathering place for most of the Cajuns these days. It wasn't like the movies, really. A precious few, like the swamp guide Half-Pint and a barmaid called Houseboat Debbie, lived full-time on their boats, but most had real houses elsewhere. The swamp was for recreation. Their everyday lives were in towns—Henderson, Breaux Bridge, Cecilia, even Lafayette. The Cajuns would leave the camps on Sunday afternoon and begin a week that I could only imagine, a world of which we were not a part.

I was born in south Georgia, grew up in Alabama, moved to Mississippi, worked years for a Tennessee newspaper, then moved to Atlanta, which I disliked. I sometimes felt as if I had no real home. Mississippi had come closest to being that anchor most of us seem to need. I love my farm in north Mississippi, but even there I have no roots. Hill people are a bit suspicious of outsiders, which you will remain no matter how long you live there if you were not born there. I've been spending time—at times, all my time—in the Iuka, Mississippi, area for more than two decades. And I still wouldn't be invited to join the Newcomer's Club if they had one. I think the distrust of outsiders in the hills harkens to a day when the best way to make a living was moonshine. Anyone who moves to town without a really good excuse is a potential revenuer, or the twenty-first century equivalent.

My own parents often sit around and rhapsodize about their hometown of Colquitt, Georgia, reminiscing about childhood and weaving genealogical tapestries that make my head spin. She was so-and-so before she married so-and-so's youngest son and became so-and-so. My friends in Iuka who are natives feel the same way about north Mississippi. Listening to some of them talk is like reading the biblical begats aloud.

I, on the other hand, had no place on my private map that felt like the county seat of my heart. That can be a good thing. It can prevent you from boring others with non-ending stories about the Good Old Days in Pleasantville. It can give you perspective and help you keep an open mind about different cultures and mores.

But one Christmas day on a houseboat in the swamp, I identified with the floating water hyacinths. They blow with the wind and visit one shore one day and another the next. The locals cuss them.

Putting Down Roots

Johnelle found the house. Of course he did. Johnelle fixes or finds everything. He knows where to look for whatever or whomever you need—a mattress, a plumber, a boat, a motor, the best boudin, the cheapest oil change. Johnelle is Henderson's fixer, its greeter, its unofficial mayor. Everyone knows him, and he knows everyone.

If you'd let him, Johnelle would choose the model and make of the car you buy, arrange your furniture in your house, landscape your yard. Reared to be polite, at first I didn't say too much when Johnelle inserted himself in my decorating or landscaping schemes. But, like Johnelle, I have strong opinions on such matters; he's not the only one who religiously watches the Home and Garden channel. We butted heads more than once on placement of stepping stones, or how to outline a flower bed, even how to arrange the living room.

"Why do you want to cover the concrete like dat?" Johnelle asked when he first saw the yard at our Georgia house. I had, with great effort, hauled in leaves and pine straw from the riverbank to disguise part of the endless pavement the previous owner evidently had wanted instead of grass. I stubbornly replaced the elaborate camouflage whenever the wind blew or the rain washed it away.

Johnelle shook his head. I was a hopeless case.

I loved the *Green Queen*. Spending time there had meant floating on more than Henderson Lake. Time on the *Queen* was truly free time, time free from telephones and newspaper editors and disgruntled readers. It was like floating through space in a protective bubble. Nobody but close friends and family knew how to reach me on the *Green Queen*. People think movie stars and millionaires and queens have impenetrable hideouts. A queen would turn green with envy for the kind of seclusion our little houseboat offered.

Despite true love for the *Queen*, I wanted a real house. Whenever we made it to Louisiana, Don spent his days in the swamp hunting ducks, and I'd explore the countryside. Occasionally I would go with Don in the late afternoons to put out his decoys for the next morning's hunt. Especially after he explained to me that placing decoys just-so was a lot like decorating a Christmas tree, I grew to enjoy the ritual. We'd sit there till twilight, witnessing some stunning swamp sunsets and waiting for the wood ducks to return to their roosts. A couple of times I even got up before the sun and made the actual hunt. I'll admit, the way Don had, almost poetically, described a duck hunt was accurate: You see things at dawn that you don't see any other time of day. Mostly, though, I left the hunting to One Duck Don.

My regional meanderings were usually solo. Don was hunting. Jeanette was working. I'd pick a destination from my stack of travel books and sling the camera strap over a shoulder. I might head for an old family bakery in Jeanerette that made superb ginger cakes, or a city called Rayne that boasted of its many frog murals painted on anything that would sit still, or an antique store housed in a defunct schoolhouse in the charming little town of Washington. Many days I would wander with no particular destination, exploring the family-owned meat markets that featured the Cajun-specialty rice sausage called boudin, or cracklins and pork rinds.

One day I happened upon a Satsuma farm, its rounded trees and bright orange fruit a stunning stretch of color. Along the way to wherever I'd end up, I admired the sumptuous landscape. With each passing trip to the swamp, I grew more determined to have a real yard in which to grow at least some of the exotic-looking plants that you see here and not elsewhere: the trumpet plants, sago palms, Christmas bells, and house-high azaleas.

MOST OF ALL, I coveted the azaleas. In late February or early March the azaleas bloom and transform the Louisiana landscape. Azaleas aren't just relegated to groomed lawns or fancy gardens. They bloom outside the doors of tire shops and mom-and-pop groceries and low-rent hovels and ordinary housing. They startle you with their rich colors and size; after I saw azaleas here I vowed never to plant any in north Mississippi. This is Azalea Country. Here they grow to the rooftops.

Not unlike Christmas, when colored lights make the pedestrian real estate dreamy, the early spring here bathes the world in Easter egg colors to die for. The old-fashioned, fuchsia-colored Formosa azaleas are my favorite, pink as a beauty queen's lips, the brightest Crayola in the box. They are everywhere. Almost. You could not grow them on a houseboat.

"Something modest," I said, "but with a big yard. A big yard with mature azaleas and maybe a live oak."

THE ORDER WAS IN, and Johnelle was on the case. One day he directed us to a dead-end street off the main route to an area I'd never seen. Surrounded by sugarcane fields, the little neighborhood was like most in Henderson—a real mix. There were house trailers, some kept neat, even manicured, and others with yards that looked hurricane-tossed. A few made Sanford & Son look like neatniks. One house had a dirt front yard with rooster huts and rabbit pens and stacks of lumber; a basketball goal was in the middle. There were Butler Buildings used as houses, and houses used as storage sheds. There were graceful palm trees in some yards, à la tourist-court Florida, and cars on cinderblocks in others. There were above-ground swimming pools and trampolines in one yard, a shrimp and seafood stand in another. It was, in essence, a circa 1950s approach to a planned community: that is, absolutely no plan at all.

Our house, the one for sale, was relatively new, but built in the old Acadian cottage style. That architecture is common here, with a steep roof and ample attic called *la garconniere,* where, used to be, the boys in a Cajun family slept. Often there's an outside stairway on the front porch leading to the attic space. There are variations on the theme—modern builders often add yucky carports—but the style is traditional and simple and pleasing to the eye.

The little house Johnelle found for sale was adorable. At least it was to us. From the outside, it might have been ten years old, which it was, or a hundred. You really could not tell. Made of redwood and circled by tall, even majestic pines, the house had been custom-built for a young shrimp fisherman and his bride. The couple planned on moving to a double-wide, which would be much larger and accommodate their growing family. I could not imagine leaving the cute cottage—with its oak floors, a claw-foot tub, lots of ingenious storage and an adequate, bright blue kitchen—for a trailer, but, lucky for us, that was their plan.

There was no live oak in the yard—we would have to plant

one; they grow remarkably fast—and no azaleas, much less mature ones. Nothing's perfect.

One late afternoon we met the young couple. Don stood in the yard and talked to the man, who was cleaning his boat. I stepped inside at the wife's invitation, just far enough to glimpse the claw-foot tub and take in all the storage space. There were no inspections, tours, return visits—and absolutely no hesitation. We agreed on a price. A closing date was set. A lawyer was found to handle the particulars; Johnelle, of course, found the lawyer. Our attorney, Johnelle belatedly explained in a conspiratorial tone, had just been released from federal prison where he'd been serving a sentence for game-law violations. Don, who had recently retired from teaching journalism at the University of Alabama in Birmingham, made the trip to Henderson for the closing. I was on assignment in Savannah, Georgia, and couldn't be there for the formalities.

Don and I had cashed savings bonds to pay for the little house, which we considered a real bargain. It was to be a cash deal. Don arrived at the lawyer's office at the appointed time and began the rigmarole that attends any house closing these days. About halfway into the paperwork, the lawyer suggested a lunch break. By now, he was holding our money, a substantial amount, at least to us, despite the reasonable price of the house.

Everyone went separate ways to eat lunch and, according to the plan, returned to the lawyer's office at one o'clock to finish the transaction. Everyone, that is, but the lawyer. Don phoned me in Savannah, where a hurricane was threatening the coast and keeping me prisoner inside a motel room. Don reported that he and the others were just sitting, waiting impatiently for the lawyer to show. I was already concerned about the hurricane; the phone call only added to my unease. I was anxious about the money, worried that perhaps a man with a prison record might cash our check, buy a really nice car, and flee for a land where you could shoot as many ducks as you wanted, the hell with Louisiana.

Hours later Don called to say the house was officially ours. The lawyer had returned, a tad drunk, but with our check intact, to finish the deal.

"Well," Don said that night in his soft Mississippi drawl. "He'd just gotten out of the pen. I guess he was entitled to celebrate."

And so, with the memorable closing behind us, the Cajun cottage was ours. Johnelle and I were both excited about decorating.

THE NEIGHBORS DIDN'T EXACTLY rush over to welcome us to the street and invite us to a block party. Our property line joined that of a family with adolescent boys. The youths raised and trained bulldogs. Dog-fighting in Louisiana is illegal but common. Law enforcement often seems to look the other way. A more recent money-making scheme involving the raising of pit bulls arises from the desire of many city gang members to parade ferocious dogs whenever they are out and about. You're only as tough as your dog, I guess.

I'm not certain what our neighbors were doing with their mean dogs, but the creatures made me extremely nervous. Only a low hurricane fence separated the dogs from us and our visitors, many of whom had young children. At any given time two or three dogs were kept in pens in a windowless utility shed. Once a day most days, when the boys came home from high school, the dogs were trotted out into the yard and tethered on heavy chains wrapped around pecan trees. Every now and then a dog would get away before it could be chained, resulting in panicky shouts and the occasional dog fight. Don once witnessed the boys using a crow bar to force two of the ferocious dogs apart.

That was the scene on one side of our house. A family of Northern transplants, a couple and their two little girls, lived directly across the street in front of us. The woman worked at a local factory; the man stayed home all day in the pale pink house. The older of the children, Katy, had a severe limp from a birth defect. She would climb down from the school bus and slowly drag her bad leg up the wooden steps to her house. I'd often watch her timidly knock on the door for a few minutes before giving up and sitting down on the stoop to draw or play. On some days she sat there for hours, entertaining herself.

I befriended Katy, who helped me decorate my Christmas tree the first year we had the house. We drew fish and mermaids and sprinkled glitter on real sand dollar ornaments. She was a quiet, creative little soul who delighted in any adult attention. In return, I was putty. Nothing seemed to please her quite as much as thinking she had helped me transform an ordinary object into one of beauty. One year our glittering fish, boats, and anchors dangled from a cedar we cut in the woods. Katy sat and stared with wide eyes, like an artist at her first gallery show who can't believe it's all happening.

One day we arrived at the Henderson house from Georgia just in time to see a U-Haul backed up to Katy's house. The family was moving away, the mother explained when I encountered her. They were going to Oklahoma where they had extended family. That weekend they staged a huge garage sale, getting rid of televisions and lamps and anything else that wouldn't fit in the U-Haul and wasn't nailed down. A lot of the merchandise, according to gossip we heard later, belonged to a rent-to-own store, not to the family at all. The neighbors left behind an avalanche of unpaid bills, including the mortgage. The bank got the house back. The family's name showed up in the local newspaper's legal advertisements for weeks afterwards.

She promised to write, but I never heard from sweet little Katy again.

IT WAS A NEIGHBORHOOD of sad stories, the kind that ride tandem with poverty and ignorance. One mid-morning I was sitting on the deck behind our house watching the birds and enjoying the quiet when suddenly I heard ferocious shouting. A neighborhood mother, who had been at work, had roared into her own driveway, jumped out of the car and begun yelling at two of her sons who looked cowed and sheepish. One, who appeared to be about ten years old, sat on the side of an inflatable swimming pool; both the child and the pool looked partially deflated. The other boy, maybe twelve, sank to his knees on the grass.

"Goddamn you, you little bastards," the mother screamed. The woman let loose a torrent of obscenities that would make a Marine take cover. I have worked in newsrooms most of my adult life and am no stranger to cursing. This woman's words would have curdled milk.

The best I could follow, a third, older son had called the mother at her work to settle an argument between his two brothers. The mother's invectives filled the sugarcane fields beyond us, and I sat still as a statue, afraid to move. I had no idea how much angrier she might get if she knew there was an audience.

"You'll be sorry for this, you little asses," she raged. "Next time you need someone to buy your goddamn cigarettes, you'll have to call somebody else. I'm done with you."

She got in the car and drove away. The boys jumped up and

went about their business. I sincerely hoped she wasn't head of the Welcome Wagon.

Behind our house, thank goodness, was the small Henderson Bible Church, a cinderblock building kept immaculate by the congregation. The church also owned the property to our west, a cemetery full of the quietest neighbors a body could want. Most everyone in Henderson is Catholic, but the few religious rebels who are not Catholics attend HBC. The church met only two or three times a week. Once, not long after we took possession of our new home, a new grave was added to the half dozen plotted in the cemetery. A high school boy had died in a car wreck. For a week or so, a stream of distraught teens visited their friend's grave one at a time. You'd see them standing there, awkwardly shifting from foot to foot, paying their respects.

Sherman Soileau, the pastor at HBC, quickly became our friend. We'd chat with him over the back fence whenever he drove up to keep office hours. We'd compliment one another on home or church improvements, unspoken gratitude in our voices that we had such neat neighbors. We'd commiserate over the heat or the mosquitoes. It was by far the most neighborly relationship we found on the street, at least at first. If there'd been a block party, we'd have run the risk of being bitten, cussed out, or converted.

We painted our white house yellow because Don had always wanted a yellow house. I preferred pink—on the coast or in Louisiana you can get away with it—but Don didn't think pink was appropriate for a duck camp. Not to mention there was already the one pink house on the block, Katy's. So pale yellow it was. I thought yellow would make a nice backdrop for pink azaleas and didn't really mind losing the debate.

I did not walk but ran to the nearest nursery in Breaux Bridge and bought half a dozen azalea plants, the biggest ones I could afford. I imagined a low-maintenance yard with mostly pine straw for a floor, and fuchsia azaleas breaking the monotony and rising into the pines. I chopped at the pine tree roots all of one day, plugging azaleas along the hurricane fence line. I also planted two pampas grass plants and a couple of sago palms. I figured it would be no time until I'd successfully hidden the neighbors' pit bulls on their chains, and the troubled trailer residence where cussing and fussing were constantly on the dial, and, for good measure if not necessity, the little church. I left "open" the fence line between our house and the cemetery, which was as pretty as a park.

I did not take into account the fact that the summer months when we'd be mostly elsewhere were the months when new plants need watering. Visit after visit I'd drive up to discover I'm the only gardener in Louisiana who cannot grow an azalea, or a sago palm. The pampas grass—which, by the way, is what Johnelle strongly suggested I should plant for a quick and sure screen—thrived. Everything else died.

What didn't die was my enthusiasm. I had seen what could grow in this muck, and I intended to have a showplace yard. It might just take a while. I bought some of the white gum boots that the shrimpers use, the white being cooler to work in than the more traditional black ones. Johnelle calls them "Catahoula Reeboks."

After two or three plantings and as many years, I finally gave up altogether on azaleas and replaced them with waxed privet, or ligustrum, which needs a lot less water and is impossible to kill. If I couldn't control my neighbors' less than fastidious habits, I could exist peacefully behind natural walls of green. Henderson's lack of zoning laws results in a free-wheeling landscape of wrecked cars, old boats used as aluminum can depositories, cocks raised for fighting beneath pyramid-shaped sheds, horses, home businesses including beauty shops, catfish and shrimp markets, and Laundromats. Near our house is a fisherman's cooperative, which, certain times of the year, employs crawfish-shellers from as far away as Mexico. The Mexicans all live together in a rental house on one end of the street. At the co-op, crawfish husks pour through a giant funnel into the back of a dump truck, a sea of red refuse. A wall of green could hide it all.

That first year, in a new homeowner hurry, Johnelle and I constantly clashed on plans for *my* yard and house. I'd bristle when he'd ignore my intentions and bully his way into the landscaping or decorating scheme. For one thing, he hated real flowers, preferring the artificial ones. I felt the opposite.

"Why you want to plant more real flowers to take care of?" he'd demand.

I'D GET ANGRY, BUT not for long. Johnelle was impossible to stay mad at. He was relentlessly a good neighbor. Legally blind from a rare genetic disease, retinitis pigmentosis, by the time we bought the house Johnelle had had to relinquish his driver's license. That didn't stop him from visiting. For a while, he traveled the few blocks from his own home on his riding lawn mower, a vision of volunteerism on the green John Deere. Then, one day he appeared at the door on a cute red scooter. With his decidedly Gallic features and ample middle, he could have been an advertisement for a Provencal tour. All he needed was a beret.

The progressive eye disease totally destroyed his peripheral vision. Riding the scooter soon became dangerous for him, too. Eventually his doctor advised Johnelle to avoid busy streets altogether, even on foot. None of that slowed him much. He once rode the Greyhound bus all the way from Louisiana to Georgia to visit us.

If a man will ride the Dog to visit you, all the way from Lafayette to Atlanta, he's a friend.

Appropriately enough, it would be our first Christmas in our new Henderson house when the Cajun definition of friendship became clear to me. The old adage about a fellow who will give you the shirt off his own back is widely quoted but, in reality, rarely illustrated.

Don and I had driven together to Henderson from Atlanta for the Christmas holidays. Our usual arrangement was to bring two cars so that Don could pull a boat to the swamp and hunt, and I could go about my own business. This time, for some reason, we'd both come in the truck. As Christmas approached, urgent phone calls penetrated the usual quiet of the swamp. My mother was in a Montgomery, Alabama, hospital with dangerous arterial blockages. Don's brother was in a Mobile hospital near death. We both needed to go to our respective family emergencies, but we had only one car.

Johnelle and Jeanette appeared. Without much ado, Johnelle dropped the keys to their only car on the table and said, "Keep it as long as you need." Jeanette, who by then was working at a Lafayette factory, could catch a ride to work, they insisted. No problem. No big deal. They literally were offering the shirt off their own back and wanted us to take it.

We could not in good conscience borrow their only car. Instead, we drove to the Mississippi Gulf Coast and rented a car, then I headed to Montgomery and Don drove on to Mobile. The long ride gave me a chance to think about the concern in those two dear faces, rare friends who didn't hesitate to inconvenience themselves to make our lives easier.

Time and again the characteristic Cajun generosity would reveal itself, bringing tears to my flinty eyes and restoring my faith in human nature. After three decades in the newspaper business, that faith had about eroded until I discovered Henderson. Friendship meant something here, and not just swapping expensive gifts at Christmas time or swapping gossip. It meant sitting up with folks who had lost a family member, giving even when it meant you would have to do without, staying in touch even if you had to ride your lawnmower to visit.

After that Christmas, I pretty much let Johnelle have his way with his interior design schemes. He made me things in his shop despite doctor's orders to avoid power tools. We went shopping in the junk stores, and he was the absolute best at thinking of one more way to rearrange too much furniture in a small space. After a time, I couldn't remember why I'd been so resistant to having his help, except for that artificial flower thing.

A Good Time Was Not
Had by All

With the house, of course, came more frequent and longer visits to Henderson, now our official second home, regulation mailbox and all. We'd finagle up to three weeks during holidays and leave Henderson reluctantly only when work or family duties called us away. Our cozy yellow house and a growing number of good Cajun friends made us feel more and more schizophrenic about our divided lives. While away from Louisiana, we'd rhapsodize to anyone who'd listen about the charms of Atchafalaya Swamp and Cajun Country. We painted as romantic a picture of the scene as Longfellow did in his epic poem *Evangeline*.

Our descriptions invited guests even when we didn't, and they'd inevitably show up when we least expected or needed them. I started dividing the steady stream of visitors into three categories, the same way I'd once, as a youth, divided all women. Women were either Scarletts or Melanies, one of two basic types. They were either independent and daring, à la Scarlett, or milquetoast and mealy-mouthed Melanies. It was a broad and unfair way to categorize women. Same goes for visitors. You can't really narrow it down to three neat groups. But there did seem to be a quickly recognizable behavioral pattern for houseguests, beyond the obvious distinctions of "invited" and "uninvited."

First, and most frequently, thank goodness, were the genuinely and intellectually curious folks who had heard about the area and wanted to know more. They did homework beforehand, knew at least vaguely what to expect and made an honest effort to absorb a little Cajun culture beyond the superficial. For the most part, they already knew of the infamous exile of French Catholics from Nova Scotia in 1755, the great Diaspora that resulted, eventually, in the relocation of many Acadian farmers to Louisiana. They had read Longfellow's *Evangeline,* if nothing else, and had a frame of reference, however romanticized it might be. That was my first broad group: The Open-Minded. They were a pleasure to host.

Then there came a category I thought of as The Surprised. They were tourists who had no clue exactly what they were coming to see, and vague interest in what they saw. I include in that group folks who owned one idea and one idea only about all of Louisiana. That idea always involved New Orleans' Bourbon Street and maybe a restored cotton plantation or two. Louisiana was a party, a hoop skirt, and not much more. The Surprised usually left Henderson quickly—and disappointed. Our town has a couple of drive-through daiquiri stands, plenty of poboy menus, and sells booze in all the filling stations and grocery stores. Other than that, it doesn't have a whole lot in common with the sophisticated Big Easy. The food here is equally delicious, but features country cooking, fried and sturdy and more basic. New Orleans, food and otherwise, is more of a Creole culture, with a broader European base.

People wanting to party New Orleans-style typically were bored with such a rural and natural scene as Henderson offers. The Surprised brought too many clothes—there's not a single

place we go around Henderson that requires fancy duds—and
felt cheated when they didn't get to wear them. They wanted
breakfast at Brennan's and got supper at Mulate's, our favorite
Cajun dance hall and watering hole. Cosmopolitan Lafayette
offers some of the things such Surprise guests wanted—fancy
restaurants, art museums, Mardi Gras krewes—but we don't
know or frequent the scene there.

There was a third and final category of visitors for which I
grew to have zero patience. They were the Prejudiced Pilgrims
who simply could not see beyond their own misconceptions,
who thought they knew more than they did, who expected to
find Cajuns kept in formaldehyde, a shy, simple people who
eschew all modern conveniences and live their lives exactly as
their ancestors did. More Amish than Cajun, really. Those mis-
guided pilgrims typically made facile judgments and left with
raised eyebrows. They saw only the poverty, not the generous
people, the litter, not the wildlife, the truck stop casinos, not
the natural beauty. They saw only the negatives, and there are
plenty of those, of course.

In fairness, they saw some of the same things that bothered,
and bother, me. I guess it's not unlike the axiom that you can
criticize your relatives but a stranger better not try. I can get in
high dudgeon about neighbors who don't bother to collect their
garbage cans between weekly pickups, but I want the casual
visitor to see beyond such slovenly habits. I guess I sometimes
want too much.

Hypocrite that I am, I have cut a neighbor's grass before
a persnickety guest was to arrive. What does that say about
me?

ONE DAY I CALLED a Lafayette newspaper columnist to ask him
a question. This journalist is knowledgeable about local history

and has even written a book on the subject, a book, by the way, that makes scant mention of Henderson. In introducing myself I mentioned that I lived in Henderson part of the year.

"Why?" he asked, then quickly laughed.

I took offense.

It's nigh impossible in a single visit to comprehend the dichotomy that is Cajun culture. On one hand, there's an increasing embrace of any and all technology by many of the Cajuns. They have been seduced by cell phones and wide-screen televisions same as all Americans. Many Cajuns also have a love affair with any contraption that makes lots of noise outdoors—four-wheelers and Harleys and jet skis. I read in the local newspaper that Louisiana motorcycle fatalities increased by more than three hundred percent from 1997 to 2003. A helmet law finally was passed in 2004 but many ignore it.

On the other hand, if you bother to look, you can still meet Henderson men who build their own pirogues and bateaus, and fishermen who prefer to make their own nets though you can buy them at the local feed store. You can meet cooks who make their own roux—the flower and grease concoction that is at the base of gumbo and most Cajun food—though Hebert's has plenty ready-made on the shelves.

And, in the region, if not in Henderson per se, the discerning visitor discovers the same economic strata you'd find almost anywhere else. Along with the extreme poverty of our town is the great wealth elsewhere. The oil millionaires of nearby Lafayette are part of the mix. Then there is, of course, the huge Cajun middle class.

A few visitors simply dismissed Cajun culture as backward without bothering to look around at all. One elderly, wealthy woman seemed to take it personally when the Cajun French she heard at a dance hall didn't match her textbook variety. She considered herself fairly fluent and had made the obligatory Grand Tour stops in Europe.

"They speak a bastardized French," she complained, "and I don't understand a single word."

Cajun French is not bastardized at all; it's an archaic French sprinkled with some English, pronouncing the final consonant in the plural forms where modern French has dropped it and exhibiting other peculiarities. Cajun French resembles the French still spoken—if not in Paris—in the countryside and villages of northern and western France.

Among our most noteworthy and appreciative visitors was a married couple, both teachers, from Normandy. Europeans, the French in particular, are frequent visitors to Cajun Louisiana, which they've read so much about. We had swapped houses with Frederic and Marie and their son, Corentin, through an internet exchange program designed for traveling on the cheap. Once we returned from Normandy, I quizzed Johnelle and Jeanette about their ability to understand the French visitors.

"We understood them when they'd speak slowly," Jeanette assured me.

Frederic repeated almost the same words in an email exchange when I posed the identical question to him. He could understand Jeanette and Johnelle's French "when they spoke slowly."

THE VISIT OF FREDERIC and Marie inspired more home improvements than have happened at our Cajun cottage before or since. I was determined that our French friends would find everything perfect and to their liking. I call them friends, though we never physically met. All of our other friends and relatives did meet the French family. I consider that a serious drawback of the house-swapping system. I was jealous that we never got to meet the, by all accounts, delightful French family.

At any rate, before we left for France and they arrived in the U.S., I furiously cleaned. I bought new bed sheets and comforters, decorated Corentin's room with an alligator mobile, and left movies and toys for him to enjoy. We built a new, old-brick front walk with Johnelle's help. I planted flowers that I was reasonably sure wouldn't last the summer, had our carpets professionally cleaned, waxed floors, and patched cracks in the sheetrock ceiling. Our old Nissan, a part of the official swap arrangement, was making a funny but harmless noise when you put it into reverse. We spent several hundred dollars to make the irritating sound go away so as not to alarm the visiting French.

We even rented a weekend houseboat for the French family in case they wanted to experience the swamp up close and personal. Don and I had reluctantly sold the *Green Queen* after buying the house, unable to justify the expense of keeping both. But I wanted Frederic and Marie and Corentin to get the full treatment, and they did. Basin Landing, among other places, rents houseboats for the weekend.

Jimmy Johnson, my former husband who remains my good friend, was one of many chums and relatives we enlisted to make sure our visitors got the royal treatment. Jimmy greeted the couple at the New Orleans airport and led them all the way to our house in Henderson, about 125 miles away. Jimmy, like everyone else who met them, was charmed by the family. He reluctantly left the jet-lagged trio that night after a brief orientation of Henderson. They were standing in a pool of artificial light and a swarm of mosquitoes, the ubiquitous pests Frederic called "moe-sqweet-toes." The next day, despite all my best efforts to make our little Henderson home comfortable and appealing and safe, Frederic stepped into a fire ant bed in the front yard. Some things you simply cannot plan for. The couple also was amazed by all the dead armadillos alongside the roadside. They called them "tattoos."

The swap was not off to an auspicious start.

I had agonized that the house exchange was to take place in July and August, traditional holiday months for the French, but an unbearably hot time in the swamp for the uninitiated. I looked it up: The median high temperature in Normandy in July was 72 degrees. I worried that Frederic and Marie would suffer from the heat and blanket-heavy humidity that settles over Louisiana for the summer. I didn't worry much about Corentin. Kids have an amazing ability to cope. In rereading some of my own pre-swap e-mails on the subject, with their emphasis on snakes, mosquitoes and brutal heat, I'm amazed I didn't talk them out of coming. I did a great job of un-selling the swap.

TURNS OUT, I NEEDN'T have worried about the climate imbalance. It was 2003, the summer of the fluke heat wave in France that killed seventy-five thousand people, especially elderly Parisians. The August day we drove to Mont Saint Michel from Frederic and Marie's house in Normandy's Briouze, the temperature was 102. The un-air-conditioned Renault overheated and had to be parked for the duration of our stay. Fortunately, Frederic had left a back-up vehicle, an older Renault.

The residents of Normandy truly suffered that summer. You could see it in their faces, if you saw any faces. Almost everyone was holed up from the relentless sun behind those elaborate French shutters in un-air-conditioned homes. The three-foot-thick walls of our house kept us cool, so long as we didn't wander outside. Frederic's father, who had endured bypass heart surgery just before the great house swap got underway, wanted to visit us during our month-long stay but never ventured out because he feared the extreme weather.

It got Louisiana-hot in Henderson, naturally, the same relentless way it does every summer. But, temperature-wise, our French visitors had the better end of the bargain. Everything in Louisiana—the automobiles, the stores, the houses, even the rental houseboat—is air-conditioned.

Our French visitors had no complaints, or, if they did, were too polite to tell us. That put them in a visitors' category all by themselves.

The French made it fine on their own. Whenever I am around to conduct tours for our visitors, though, I usually start in the town of St. Martinville, the parish seat, also known as Petit Paris. It's an exceptionally pretty town, and at its center is a grand edifice the color of eggshells, old St. Martin de Tours Church. The aristocrats who fled Paris after the French Revolution, as well as the displaced Acadian farmers, had great influence on the community.

Though the Cajuns are the most famous French descendents in this part of Louisiana, they are not the only ones. French settlers were here long before the Cajun exiles came at the invitation of a Spanish government. And, later, after the French Revolution, other Frenchmen made Louisiana home. Also in this part of the state are people with African, German, and Anglo roots.

A statue of Evangeline that looks like the movie star Delores del Rio is just outside the cream-colored church. The actress modeled for the statue after playing Evangeline in the 1929 movie of the same name. The life-size maiden sits atop the grave of Emmeline Labiche, said to be the inspiration for Longfellow's famous poem.

In these parts, Longfellow's Evangeline is namesake for

everything from auto parts stores to oak trees to oil fields. You can't swing a dead cat without hitting an Acadian maiden.

So with visitors in tow, I start at the church, with its spooky grotto inside, and the Evangeline tombstone, and the so-called Evangeline oak on the Bayou Teche. The oak is supposed to be the meeting place of Emmeline Labiche and Louis Arceneaux, her Gabriel counterpart.

My favorite St. Martinville tour stop, though, is the Petit Paris Museum, run by the church ladies, which has homemade gifts on the first floor and, upstairs, a collection of Mardi Gras costumes. The costumes are mostly from one year, 1984, when the town's theme for Mardi Gras was the legendary spider wedding. The story of the wedding is fanciful enough to impress any willing tourist with half an ounce of romance in her soul.

Legend has it that a local antebellum sugarcane planter, Charles Durand, who came from France around 1820, threw a spectacular wedding for his twin daughters, who quite conveniently managed to marry on the same day. Durand, the story goes, was a spider enthusiast. He collected spiders from the swamp near Catahoula and days before the wedding carefully deposited them in the oaks and pines that lined the three-mile-long drive to the Big House. On the morning of the marriages, Durand supposedly supplied his slaves with bellows full of silver and gold dust. Over a canopy of cobwebs, the dust was sprinkled. The obliging spiders had spun the webs strategically and right on schedule. It did not rain. Thousands of people from up and down Bayou Teche attended, and the couples left for their New Orleans honeymoons on boats that steamed up the bayou to fetch them.

I know what you're thinking: new money. I'd say Durand was flaunting his wealth, but with great panache. If the legend is even half true, he had flair, not to mention a love of symmetry. He was married twice; his first wife died. With each woman he had twelve children, supposedly to avoid being unfair to either lady.

The Spider Wedding Mardi Gras costumes are to die for. There are glittery webs in the skirts of frothy dresses. There are black velvet spiders hanging in hats and parasols and bouquets. There are, of course, two brides, two ring-bearers, two of everything. It's a kind of Doublemint, double-your-pleasure, double-your-fun, fantasy wedding party. The museum display sure makes you wish more of today's brides were a tad more creative. If only they'd get away from cloying colors and sickeningly sweet themes and use a fresh approach. An alligator wedding, for instance, would be novel and oh-so appropriate. Attendants could wear skin boots and leopard print dresses. The punch could be frog green. It might not make *Southern Living*, but another legend would be born. A century from now some small town would be inspired to adopt the Alligator Wedding as its Mardi Gras theme.

I once dreamed that I attended the Durand wedding, rode that lane beneath a canopy of shimmering spider webs. I drank champagne—you just know there had to be French champagne—from flutes shipped from Paris especially for the occasion.

Then I wrote about the scene for a New Orleans newspaper, impressing upon my dear readers the expert and lively mixture of arachnids and sugar money.

The Tool Shed Reading Club

I quit my Atlanta newspaper columnist's job in 2001. The money was good, the position prestigious. The newspaper, *The Atlanta Journal Constitution*, was the most editorially liberal I'd ever worked for, and that being the case, its owner liked both me and my politics. To give up the newspaper salary and keep only the syndication would reduce my salary by nine-tenths, literally.

Quitting was the easiest decision I ever made in my professional life.

I had arrived in Atlanta as a columnist in 1994, exactly one month after the wildly popular Lewis Grizzard died. The newspaper, though shrewd enough not to bill me as his replacement, put my column in the same bit of journalistic real estate Grizzard had left empty. Grizzard was a political conservative, a University of Georgia graduate, a humorist and a man. I was a liberal, an Auburn graduate, not a humorist, and not a man. It seemed as if most of his fans wanted the column space left blank indefinitely, or at least filled by a Grizzard wannabe; there are plenty of those. If only I'd saved my angry mail from that first year in Atlanta I would have had an effortless book: *Grizzard Is Dead and I Don't Feel So Good Myself.*

After a couple of years in the column spot, though, I managed to find my kind of readers, or rather they found me. I rediscovered my home state of Georgia in the process, column by column, driving from town to town in the only way I knew to keep a running commentary interesting. I loved most parts of the state, but never managed to warm up to the capital city that dominated it. All my best-laid plans to reconnect with college chums and relatives who had settled in Hot 'Lanta quickly died in the face of logistics. It took hours to get from one part of the city to another, and by day's end I was relieved just to get home. Going out again to face more traffic jams or parking hassles was not even possible; I was always bone-tired. There had to be monumental motivation to make me drive back into the fray in the evenings. As a result, the city's plays and art exhibits and first-run movies and concerts were nothing to me. I might as well have stayed in Mississippi. And, most days, I wished I had.

After I had been six years on the job, another Atlanta columnist, the iconic Celestine Sibley, died. Editors moved my column to her vacant spot. Here we go again, I thought. I dreaded hearing from her six decades' worth of fans. This time, however, it was a far better fit, a smoother transition; Celestine had more thoughtful fans, and now readers at least had heard of me and knew my work. And, we were both women. But by this time I was physically and emotionally tired. I hated the horrendous traffic I was forced to deal with daily, and the relentlessness of four columns a week was working on my psyche. I no sooner finished one piece than another was due. My cartoonist friend Charles Schulz best described the deadline business when he said, "It's like running up a glass hill."

I'd been running up a glass hill for nearly thirty years. I wanted off.

I struck a deal with my syndicate, King Features, to write one general interest column a week. For the first time in my adult life—with the exception of thirteen months when in desperation I took an editing job for the State of Mississippi—I was not working for a newspaper. It was dizzying, almost, having time for the first time to go to leisurely lunches with girlfriends, or to spend a day putting photographs in a scrapbook. I loved having a day here and there to work in the yard, or to write a real and rambling letter. I was broke but happier, a lot like my Henderson friends who seemed always to put leisure time over big salaries, staying home over mandatory travel. I had learned that lesson from them, and well.

When I decided to quit, we immediately put the nice, roomy Atlanta-area house on the market. The house had kept me sane during the Atlanta years. It was surrounded by a farmer's four hundred acres and cozy to the Little Tallapoosa River. We could drop the canoe into the river in our backyard and float ten miles without seeing another house.

The house, with its idyllic setting, sold in one week. I hurriedly shoe-horned our furniture and most of our belongings into the one-bedroom home in north Mississippi and proceeded to sit back and enjoy life. And enjoying life, for us, by now, meant spending lots of time in Louisiana. Freed from Atlanta, and with Don already retired, we now could spend entire winters in Henderson.

A SNAGGLE-TOOTHED GIRL NAMED Carly and her brother Sam had moved into the pink house across the street from us in Henderson. It was Katy's former house and at first I swore I wouldn't get attached to more street urchins who might or might not stay around. Carly lived there with her mother and the mother's boyfriend who had three children, not to mention grandchildren, who frequently visited. I tried to ignore them all. But kids, especially when fate places them so close, are hard to ignore. One morning little Sam was kneeling by an injured baby bird next to our gate. He was stroking the bird's head and trying to feed it.

We drove off on some errand or another, but when we returned I saw Sam in his yard and asked after his bird.

"I killed it," he said matter-of-factly. "He was biting me with his nose."

Sam was like that. A bit surly, no-nonsense, but smart and funny. One Christmas day we were watching out the window as Sam tried out his new go-cart, zooming around the block, into the gravel church parking lot behind us. He wrecked, of course, turning the machine upside down in the gravel, breaking his arm and spending the rest of Christmas in surgery.

Carly was shy at first. She'd come over to play with our yellow dog Mabel, squealing when the oafish puppy would jump up on her and lick her face. She had a dog, too, and one day I asked Carly what its name was.

"I already told you that," she said. Thus ended the conversation. Later, I recalled she had in fact about six months before told me the ugly pug's name was Nos.

Carly had black, worried, hound dog eyes. She could stare a hole through you and usually get her way by saying nothing. She loved for me to read aloud to her. I started bringing children's books from Mississippi to share with Carly. She was a bit hyper, as are most children these days, so I'd try and plan an art project for her to work on while I read. It was simply beyond her to sit perfectly still and listen. So she would color or paste while I read aloud from *Charlotte's Web* or *Because of Winn-Dixie.*

Carly would sometimes argue with the plot of the story, a reassuring sign that she was indeed listening while running from room to room looking for art supplies or more cookies.

"I don't get why she named the dog Winn-Dixie just because she was in that store," Carly said in typical contrariness. "It's not a good dog name at all." I started to ask what she would have named the dog, but thought better of it. She'd probably already told me.

THUS BEGAN OUR PATTERN. Carly would get home from school and rush inside her own home to do her homework as her mother insisted. But by four o'clock every weekday she was at my house, ready for reading, art, and a snack. The art work usually involved glitter and glue, and soon a sparkling patina covered everything in the house. Tired of vacuuming daily, I suggested we move out to the almost-empty tool shed. Carly agreed. Children love small spaces.

By now Carly was bringing her friends and relatives to the after-school event. On a regular basis there was Allyson, a doe-eyed beauty who had her own cell phone. Toby and Taylor, the boyfriend's grandchildren, started showing up. And Sam was a regular. When it grew cold in the tool shed, I suggested we move back into the house.

"No!" Carly insisted. "We're the Tool Shed Reading Club. We have to be in the tool shed."

Henderson had no library. The nearest one was about eight miles away in Cecilia, much too far for latchkey kids to visit on their own. I wrote a column about the Tool Shed Reading Club in my backyard, making the name official, and the idea fascinated lots of people. Strangers from as far away as Knoxville, Tennessee, left books in a box on our Henderson porch. Mississippi and Alabama friends sent stacks of books their children had outgrown. Reporters from newspapers around the South contributed. A woman in Florida offered thousands of books to the town if it could find a place to house them. What had begun to amuse Carly was the genesis of a Henderson town library.

A Mississippi friend, Anne Holtsford, made a special trip down to Henderson to help me fix up the tool shed, which, much to Don's chagrin, was becoming less of one every day. I'd let the kids gradually push the shovels, saws, and duck decoys to the back of the building, leaving more space for their artwork and books. Anne and I hung a bamboo blind with parrot lights above it. We could drop it ceremoniously whenever the Reading Club was in session, hiding the "ugly stuff," as the children called the tools and hunting paraphernalia. Anne, who is artistic, painted a sign for the front of the building, and we held a grand unveiling with the children present. We recovered an old sofa with a bright, striped tablecloth and used plastic flower placemats for seat cushions. Colorful lamps, a Snoopy clock and flea market rugs added to the look, something like the attic in *Little Women*. Best of all were the books, which now filled a used white bookcase and several long shelves across the length of the room. People kept sending us books, beautiful books, with the marvelous illustrations that you don't get anywhere else. The children worked on clever bookmarks to send as a thank you for the donations.

I let the children check out the books to take home, carefully writing down the book's name and specifying when it should be returned. Our membership understood more about the checking-out than the return process. Few books were returned. That was all right, too. At least they were in the hands of children—and being read.

Allyson, a strikingly precocious little girl, read aloud better than anyone else, including me. Until you've heard Allyson read *Davy Deer's New Red Scarf* in her lilting Cajun accent and with appropriate and dramatic pauses, you haven't lived. She arrived one day in a simple white T-shirt that she'd decorated herself with Magic Marker: "I Heart the TSRC," the shirt said on one side. Only the "heart" was drawn, not written. On the other side was her name. Allyson's sweet and earnest effort inspired me to get T-shirts customized for all the regulars. The shirts were yellow like the shed. Our logo was a bookworm.

SAM PRETENDED HE WASN'T that interested in the clubhouse that the others took so seriously. He was older. He was beyond cool. He didn't like girls or school. But almost every day he'd arrive, late but somehow available. He'd squeeze into a chair at the bare board of a table where we were painting or making sand-dollar necklaces or gluing together Popsicle sticks to make little sleds. Before you knew it, Sam was working intently, just as involved as the other children.

You can learn a lot about kids when you spend hours with them in such a tight space. They snuggle against you with freshly washed hair, or running noses, that intoxicating blend of need and love that only children radiate. I heard from them guileless reports about divorces, debts, drinking, stepparents, and house repossessions. Toby's mother, still in her teens, was in drug rehab. He and his brother soon moved in with his grandfather and Carly and Sam across the street. On Christmas day the reading club boys all rode over to show me the new bicycles Santa had brought them. Except for Toby; he was riding his old one.

Of all the children, Toby touched me the most. He had curly brown hair and saucer eyes and a quick grin. He seemed almost resigned to the endless shuffle between grandparents and parents. He never complained and always gave me optimistic reports on his mother. She was better. She was due home. She was going to go to school. She was back in rehab.

Sam was Toby's Fonzi, his James Dean, the ultimate hero. Toby would run to the clubhouse, eager to begin whatever games or craft I had planned for the day. When Sam arrived, late as usual, Toby would rush to show Sam whatever we were doing.

"Look, Sam," Toby would say. "We are painting flower pots for Mother's Day."

Sam would snort and grumble and say something sarcastic to a crestfallen Toby. Then, inevitably, Sam would settle down and begin his own version of the daily project, satisfying Toby that the task, whatever it was, was acceptable for he-men.

Toby never volunteered to read aloud, but one day, when I asked, he started to read in a small voice. I was amazed. His reading ability was far beyond that of most of the other children, with the possible exception of Allyson. In the tight and friendly confines of the tool shed, he was a bright, enthusiastic boy, happily making a flower pot or necklace or bookmark for his missing mother.

The ever-changing members of the Tool Shed Reading Club broke my heart on a weekly basis. Some days a pathetic story worked its way out as the kids made valentines, or played dodgeball. One day a rare verbal fight ensued, and someone called someone else's father a deadbeat, who retorted, "Yeah, well, your dad's been to jail," and then all hell broke loose. It didn't take much imagination to see they were repeating verbatim the slurs and accusations they'd heard from the sundry adults who populated their little lives. It killed me to hear it.

The membership of the Tool Shed Reading Club began staying around until dark, refusing to leave until I cooked up a big pot of macaroni and cheese for them. Don got used to the routine, too, which basically each weekday involved a house full of children when we had none of our own. Don was a sport.

And I knew deep down that the fall and winter of 2003 and 2004 were special, that there would never be another time exactly like it. I got tired of the mess and considerable expense occasionally, yet I savored every moment. I knew that if I'd still been working for a newspaper, any newspaper, I'd never have had the time to devote to this tool shed full of hapless little rascals. And I knew that I'd gotten far more out of the experience than they had.

WHEN WE LEFT HENDERSON for the summer, I didn't worry too much. The children of Henderson—unlike most kids today—played outside during the warm months. Watching them was like going back in time to my own childhood, when everything outside was better than anything inside. An ice cream truck even rolls through Henderson during the warm months, something I hadn't seen—or heard—since I was small. Again, the sight and sound harkened to the 1950s, part of the town's trademark appeal. I rightly reasoned the kids wouldn't miss the clubhouse or the books that much while I was in north Mississippi for the summertime. But I figured come fall and cool weather, they'd be ready to read in their colorful tool shed once again.

The pink house—Katy's house, Sam's and Carly's house, sometimes Toby's house—was jinxed. I'm sure of it. When we made a visit in mid-summer to check on things, we found chaos where order had been. The pink house, invitingly land-scaped by the mother, now looked abandoned. Litter was in the yard, and the flowers and shrubs she had planted were neglected. If ever a house looked as if a woman was missing, this was one. Not since Katy's father threw the carcass of the Thanksgiving turkey in the yard for the stray dogs had things looked this rough.

Carly's mother had left the pink house, taking her belongings and kids and moving into a travel trailer at a nearby RV park. I rode over to see them.

It had been too much, the young woman said, working full-time and taking care of her own children and her boyfriend's children and grandchildren as well. She planned on staying in the travel trailer until she saved enough money to buy a house.

The boyfriend, eager to save the relationship with his girlfriend, sent his own children and grandchildren to their mothers and also moved to the RV park. I never was sure where any of the other children landed. The pink house sold again. Once I saw Allyson shopping with her grandmother at the Breaux Bridge Wal-Mart. We hugged necks and Allyson explained that she might not be visiting her father in the near future as he had an out-of-town job. The grandmother offered no extra information. I haven't seen Allyson since.

The attrition was insurmountable. The children scattered like BBs on linoleum. The Tool Shed Reading Club disbanded.

And yet I still can't bring myself to roll up the blue rug and give away the few remaining books. Freewheeling art work still hangs on a string across the middle of the shed, and Don's picks and shovels are still in the back behind the Magic Screen. And some afternoons when the school bus passes, I half expect to see the children running toward their clubhouse, ready to debate the merits of *Madeline* and cream-filled oatmeal cookies. Macaroni and cheese makes me cry.

Plate Lunches by the Pound,
Heartaches by the Score

He only met Hank Williams once, but once was enough. It was 1951. D. L. Menard was nineteen. A brief exchange with the musical master changed the disciple's life.

Hank Williams was booked by the Club Teche in New Iberia, a lively, lusty town on the Bayou Teche about thirty miles south of Henderson. New Iberia perhaps is best known for being near Avery Island, a salt dome, not an island at all, which is the home of Tabasco, that gold standard of hot sauce. In recent years, New Iberia has become popular with literary pilgrims who come looking for novelist James Lee Burke's detective character Dave Robicheaux and his colorful haunts.

Robicheaux is made up. D. L. Menard is real.

In the 1950s, clubs and honky-tonks were scattered throughout the cane fields and at each of the Atchafalaya Basin landings. Even little Henderson was home to half a dozen night spots, some perched on the levee and others situated along the bridge at the "borrow" canal—the canal ditch was dug to "borrow" land for the levee that parallels it—the Bayou Amy.

Young D. L. was already performing country music, Hank's music, singing in English in his uncle's band at many of those clubs. When he heard Hank Williams was to appear in New Iberia, an eager D. L. arrived early from his home in Erath hoping to talk to his idol. Fate pivots on fine points. The brief audience with his hero happened just before the show. Hank, as you would hope to hear, was both friendly and encouraging. Not unlike his music, Hank's advice was succinct and profound, imparting a lot in very few words.

"He told me, 'Sing about things you do every day,'" D. L. said. That's it. Short and sweet. Even after fifty years, the moment moves D. L. He knows those few words made a difference.

In the course of a long newspaper career in the Deep South, and growing up mostly in Alabama, I have met many people who knew Hank, or claimed to know him, or who sang in his band, or who sat next to him in a Montgomery junior high school, or who met him on the road. But D. L. may be the only one I've interviewed whose life was completely changed, who read and remembered Hank's utterances like they were red words in the New Testament. That night long ago D. L. became Paul on the road to Damascus.

When he told me that story, D. L. was sitting in a darkened theater. Known as a jokester and storyteller as well as an ace musician, D. L. has an extensive repertoire. But this personal story may be his best. It was just after the annual Hank Williams Tribute show at the old Liberty Theater in Eunice. Most Saturday nights the Liberty is home to the *Rendez-Vous des Cajuns*, a live radio show that reminds you a lot of the Grand Ole Opry, only performed mostly in Cajun French. Once a year, however, on the January Saturday nearest the anniversary of the singer's death, a live show celebrates Hank Williams. It's all Hank, all night. Don and I try to make the annual event, and we have five times.

D. L. finished his story by stating the obvious: he took

Hank's advice to heart. *Mais oui,* as a Cajun would say. But of course! Why wouldn't a beginning singer take Hank's advice and run with it? D. L. Menard from that day on would sing about his everyday life, just as Hank had suggested. And with D. L.'s life, there's a lot to sing about.

He picked cotton before he picked a guitar. He worked the sugarcane fields and grew up poor like most of his neighbors in little Erath, about an hour's drive southwest of Henderson on the Vermillion River. His folks spoke French at home, but that language was forbidden at school. So D. L. dropped out of school. Sadly, that is a typical story for a whole generation of Cajuns. When you are made to feel ashamed of the way you talk, of your first language, it's not likely you're going to become a scholar. One historian conducted a semi-scientific survey of the Cajun population in Louisiana and Texas. For a certain generation, the insults and occasional punishments meted out by xenophobic teachers who forbade Cajun French in school made an indelible impression, even to the point of self-loathing.

As a kid, D. L. listened to the strong-signal country stations near Del Rio, Texas, and to Shreveport's KWKH, radio home of the Louisiana Hayride, the show that first gave Hank Williams wide exposure. But D. L. was sixteen before he heard a single song on the radio sung in French. Now Cajun youngsters can tune into Eunice's KBON radio, 101.1 on the FM dial, an independently owned station that devotes eighty-five percent of its play time to Louisiana musicians. There's also a Lafayette AM station (960) that calls itself The Gator and plays a mix of French and English music all day long. Lafayette's public radio station, of course, features much Cajun fare, including the live broadcast of *Rendez-Vous des Cajuns.*

In the 1950s, however, before Cajun culture and its music

became a white hot commodity, French singing simply wasn't heard on the radio. Cajun children heard it at home, or at community parties called fais do-dos, but that was different. French music was not sanctioned by the Outside, largely Anglo-Saxon World.

D. L. ordered his first guitar from Montgomery Ward for eleven dollars, postage included. Six months later he was playing and singing with a band—but still only in his second language, English.

It was Hank, D. L. told me, who first gave him artistic "permission" to sing in French. During that ten-minute meeting in New Iberia, Hank declared any and all regional music worthy of recording, and D. L. made note of that as well. If Hank gave the thumbs-up to French lyrics, the teachers could go to hell. D. L. began singing in French as often as in English, and he never forgot Hank's role in that. D. L. even took the "first few notes" of Hank's famous "Honky Tonk Blues" for his own French blockbuster, "La Porte d'en Arriere," or "The Back Door,"

By necessity, music remained a sideline for D. L. Menard. He was pumping gas in 1962 when he wrote "The Back Door," recording it as a souvenir for his seven children. Most music historians would agree that song has surpassed all but "Jolie Blonde" and Hank's "Jambalaya" as a feel-good Cajun anthem. The lively song describes the misadventures of a drinker and carouser forced to sneak into his home through the back door in the wee hours. The rascal, verse by verse, makes all his entrances, even to jail, by way of the back door. Whenever the song plays, a smile crosses the face of everyone fortunate enough to understand the French lyrics. Those of us who understand only the word "honky-tonk" smile, too; the sound of D. L.'s voice and the lively beat are reason enough. You can hear it a thousand times and still grin.

The song became an instant Cajun classic. Even after that mega hit and a string of other originals, music for D. L. was a glorified hobby, albeit his passion. Until relatively recently, and with a few notable exceptions, Cajun music was relegated to the region. D. L. and his late wife, Lou Ella, for decades ran a chair factory in Erath, making the signature ash furniture by hand.

It was a 1973 National Folk Festival in Virginia that introduced D. L. Menard to a much broader audience. Since then he has taken his unique blend of traditional country and Cajun French to thirty-six countries. In 1994 Hillary Clinton presented him with the National Heritage Fellowship Award, making official what Hank knew instinctively so long ago: regional recordings have merit.

D. L. MENARD IS OFTEN called the "Cajun Hank Williams" and does sound a little like Hank would have if Hank had had a Cajun accent. But D. L. is nobody's impersonator. He is an original. In his seventies now, he has a solid, handsome face, curly gray hair, and generous ears that look meant to support his cowboy hat. He's apt to spend part of his time on the annual Hank tribute show, or at any show, telling a funny story, sometimes in French, sometimes in English, sometimes in both.

D. L. is only one participant in the amazing two-hour Hank tribute show. There is Terry Huval, an excellent musician and organizer who came up with the idea, and Hugh Harris of Denham Springs, Louisiana, who actually has a degree in Country Music—Yes, Virginia, there is such a thing—from Northeast Mississippi Junior College. By day, Hugh is a prison guard at Angola. But it is his sideline, channeling Hank, which, of course, has made him a minor celebrity in these parts.

The national Hank revival of recent years—Super Bowl commercials featuring his music, artsy tribute albums, et cetera—has thrilled those of us who love his music. A revival wasn't necessary around Henderson. Enthusiasm for Hank in south Louisiana never waned. Hank worship has remained an integral part of Louisiana life through the decades. Hank Williams is not just remembered; he is beloved. Partly because he got his start in Louisiana, partly because he wrote the classic "Jambalaya," and maybe even partly because he married a Louisiana beauty queen, Billie Jean Jones. But the main reason Hank reigns is because so many here know and revere good music.

Music is essential to the Cajun culture. That is my single favorite thing about the area. Music is not background noise, but a constant heartbeat. Music oozes from the pores of the place, showing up live when you least expect it. Hunter Hayes, who as a precocious blond preschooler in the early 1990s amazed national television audiences playing the Cajun accordion, is the son of a Henderson boat mechanic who sometimes works on Don's outboard. The same kid who wowed a Jay Leno audience might be seen buying candy at Hebert's in Henderson.

PAT'S WHARF RESTAURANT, ABOUT a mile from our house, is home of the Atchafalaya Club, probably the biggest music and dance hall I've ever seen. The first Henderson mayor, Pat Huval, boasts that fifteen hundred people can socialize in the Atchafalaya Club without alarming the fire marshal. Most Friday nights there you can hear Steve Riley and the Mamou Playboys, international stars from a younger generation of Cajun musicians. So even in Henderson, too small for a Wal-

Mart or a movie theater, you can hear performers who have thrilled audiences around the world with Cajun music.

In a list of cultural priorities, I'd say live music is at the top, or at least on a level with food. It would take a lifetime to explore all the opportunities, and I may die trying. I had read about one dance hall in several newspapers, a venerable institution called Fred's Lounge in Mamou near Opelousas. Fred's Lounge is open only on Saturdays from 8 A.M. till 1 P.M., and a radio show is broadcast live from the small corner bar.

I got there late: 10 A.M. The joint was packed, and it might have been midnight instead of ten in the morning. The party was at full tilt. Best I could tell, once you opened the door and walked inside, you were standing on the dance floor. Everyone was dancing, including the octogenarian waitress. A waiter wore a Fred's Lounge shirt that instructed customers not to stand on the tables. Too bad that was a rule, because that was the only place left to stand. At 1 P.M. the lights were doused, and everyone walked across the street to another joint.

I cannot imagine becoming a regular at Fred's Lounge, but then I'm not as young as I used to be. I'll admit to looking around at the live music opportunities and thinking from time to time, "Why couldn't I have discovered this place before I was thirty? Or at least before I turned forty?" Back when I had stamina and was lean and mean. Too many times these days I'm content simply to have the lively mix of KBON playing on the kitchen radio while I contemplate my next meal. Down here, of course, that takes stamina, too.

BEYOND THE CULINARY ODDITIES that always make the newspaper and magazine travelogues—things such as sucking crawfish heads and eating fried gator meat on a stick—there are the less flamboyant but no less tasty staples that don't show up at festivals and tourist haunts. The best dish I've ever eaten, for instance, was Jeanette's smothered turtle. Étoufée is French for "to smother," and long ago that meant literally to cook an animal while it was still alive, thus assuring its freshness.

Crawfish étoufée was "invented," if you will, in the early 1930s at a hotel restaurant in Breaux Bridge. Cookbooks from the 1950s detailed the popular local dish, which local historians claim went a long way toward popularizing Cajun cooking. It's not so much what you eat here, but how it's prepared. The lowly meatball, for example, takes on new life when seasoned with jalapenos and secret spices by Hebert's grocery store.

You almost have to work at it to find bad food. Every grocery, every country meat market, even the ubiquitous sno-ball stands—they all serve delicious plate lunches. If the Cecilia Piggly Wiggly charged for its plate lunch by the pound, we'd be broke after a month of eating its generous helpings of take-out.

MY FAVORITE PLACES COMBINE the music and the food. Mulate's of Breaux Bridge bills itself as the original Cajun dance hall. I don't know about that, but it's hard to beat. With live music every night of the year except Christmas, the establishment lists its famous visitors in the entrance to reassure incoming patrons they are in good company. If Bob Dylan doesn't impress you, maybe Mickey Mantle will. Ron Howard, Meg Ryan, Bill Bradley, and Stephen Begley of the Royal London Ballet have all eaten and danced at Mulate's, to list but a few hungry celebrities. I'm making an assumption on the dancing part; maybe they are like Don and me, conspicuous non-dancers. Johnelle and Jeanette don't dance, either, incidentally. Even if I were a good dancer, I might hesitate to hop to my size nines at Mulate's. This is, after all, a place with adult-sized bronze shoes on the wall. It's a little intimidating for amateurs like us to waddle away from our étoufée and mix it up with the *real* dancers.

The first time I ever visited Mulate's I was depressed out of my skull. It was not a good time in my life, and I was grieving. Don, who had been to Mulate's before, kept insisting that a visit to the ultimate Cajun dance hall would make me feel better. We went. It did.

Cypress beams from Atchafalaya Swamp are covered with thousands of business cards. You look up and see a forest of professional ambition. It would make a great joke to call, say, a plumber and tell him you saw his card at Mulate's. The dance hall's lighting is just right, not dark but friendly. Cypress trunks are holding up the ceiling. It's a little like being in an air-conditioned swamp.

When we arrived that first visit, the band already was playing. The band on duty had the usual complement of Cajun accordion, fiddle, drum, guitar, and plaintive vocalist. As the first note of each song sounded, couples appeared on the wooden dance floor, a big empty spot in the restaurant's center. The expert dancers came in all ages and sizes. Women danced with young boys or with each other. Mature couples whirled about the floor with a grace that belied their age. Stout men and gray-haired grannies became elegant, seamless dance partners you could not keep your eyes off. Fathers whirled their daughters about the floor in a Cajun waltz. Some were so smooth they seemed to be rolling across the room on ball bearings.

I've been back to Mulate's possibly a hundred times. I've seen a wedding on the dance floor, heard a three-year-old drummer playing competent rhythm with his father's band, experienced enough *joie de vivre* to choke an Alabama Baptist. But I've never forgotten the sweet, happy feeling that came over me that first time. It was as if I had arrived in a heaven for sinners. This was unadulterated fun, sensory overload of unbridled, uninhibited pleasure.

Mulate's has a purity of spirit, an authenticity, which transcends food and drink and even dancing. The management has principles and sticks to them. They will not, for instance, serve crawfish until crawfish are actually in season. You won't find frozen or Chinese crawfish at Mulate's. No way, no how. And every visitor, whether Jessica Lange or Joe Boudreaux, is treated the same, with friendliness but no deference.

The customer base is equal parts tourist and local. I have tried almost everything on the menu by now, but my favorite dish is called the "half and half," which is half fried crawfish tails and half crawfish étoufée. When the crawfish isn't in season, the "half and half" is fried shrimp and shrimp étoufée. Either way, it's a winner.

Mulate's is such a treat, in fact, we usually save it for company. We try not to go too often for fear it could become routine. Fat chance. I could eat at Mulate's every night, but then I'd find my way onto the list of celebrities by virtue of being the obese woman who had to be cut out of her house on *The Jerry Springer Show*.

THEY CALL LOUISIANA THE Pelican State, but only because I wasn't in charge of naming it. I think Louisiana should be known henceforth and forever more as the Plate Lunch State. There are more funky, blue highway blue plate specials in south Louisiana than anywhere else on earth.

Every day I try somewhere new. In Cecilia, I sample the chicken fettuccine at Glenda's Creole Restaurant, a charming, one-room shack by the side of the aptly named Bayou Teche. "Teche" is an Indian word for snake. Glenda offers not one, but four entrees each day, not to mention the fried seafood and catfish that's always available. The menu is so crowded it looks like a page of begats from a small-print Bible.

I complimented Glenda on the inviting picnic tables beneath a tree outside; the last time I had stopped there was nowhere to sit and I balanced a stuffed pork chop with fixings on the hood of my truck. Glenda doesn't go for frills, only good food.

"One of my customers brought those to me, honey," Glenda said. "I have some really faithful customers."

No doubt.

I can't stay away too long from a dumpy cabin of a place named Chicken on the Bayou, the place we first heard Hélène's singing. It's right by the noisy interstate and situated behind a big, boring seafood chain restaurant that almost hides Chicken on the Bayou. Connected to the Chicken is a series of tacky, ramshackle buildings, little add-ons and extensions that once were antique stores, praline emporiums, or who-knows-what, which all somehow grew out of the restaurant like conjugations of a weak verb. You cannot judge a poboy restaurant by its exterior. Or its interior, for that matter. The tacky souvenirs you can buy run from a sponge alligator that "grows" when dropped in water to Viagra-brand hot sauce. Holes are cut in the center of each table and filled with a plastic bucket for the crawfish shells and other trash. I don't find that arrangement particularly appetizing, but the food overcomes all. The French poboy bread at the Chicken is excellent, and the crawfish tails and oysters to die for.

And then there's Poche's Meat Market near Cecilia, the working man's choice for daily sustenance. You walk through a buffet lunch line and make your choices, from rabbit to étoufée, which are heaped by generous servers into a Styrofoam tray with lid. Those of us who don't do much heavy lifting could lunch off of that single tray for an entire week. Poche's features barbecue chicken on Sundays—a Cajun culinary tradition. The take-out meat lockers at Poche's are full of tempting choices: pork roast stuffed with pork, pork chops stuffed with pork, chickens stuffed with pork, boudin sausage stuffed with everything, including crawfish. There's also the infamous *turduchen*—a hen inside a duck inside a turkey. Wretched excess.

To complicate culinary matters, every year soon after the new year, before dieting resolutions can be made, the bakeries— every little town has one—start baking King Cakes, that Mardi Gras staple that brings out the competitive nature in bakers the way Talladega tickles the ego of fast drivers.

Because of liability—someone swallowed and sued—most King Cakes now put the obligatory, symbolic plastic baby to the side of the cake, in plain view, for the hostess to hide. Traditionally, the guest who finds the baby in her cake must host the next party or, at the least, buy the next King Cake.

I have tried a praline cream cake from Poupart's Bakery in St. Martinville, which was excellent. I sampled one with strawberry filling from a chain grocery, which was good. I've been making a regular science project of it, eating my way from Bavarian cream to pecan praline. But I must say so far I prefer the hometown, T-Sue cake, the one with cream cheese filling. Best of all, T-Sue is so sure his customers have walking-around sense that he still hides the baby inside the cake where it should be. His warning is pasted on the box top: *Plastic baby inside; harmful if swallowed.*

Saint Jeanette
and the Simple Life

J eanette Latiolais is a saint. Or she should be. Next time the Catholics are looking high and low for qualified candidates, I nominate her. The miracle the church rules require could be that she's lived with Johnelle for more than four decades, or that she's been a good friend to an outsider like me.

Jeanette grew up a farmer's daughter in Henderson, right on the land where she and Johnelle and her brothers and sister and sons and mother-in-law all live now. It's no longer a farm, but a little subdivision filled with family houses, neat yards divided between her siblings and offspring and in-laws.

Despite the hard work of both her growing-up and adult years, Jeanette has the milky complexion and unlined eyes of a pampered city woman, plus that enviable salt-and-pepper hair that "mature" models in magazines always have. She is beautiful inside and out, with a beatific smile that never wavers. All the men are in love with Jeanette.

She has worked at the defunct Fruit of the Loom plant in St. Martinville, small factories in Henderson and Lafayette, the marina where we first met and now, part-time, at Henderson's M&M Sporting Goods, the Algonquin Round Table of local sportsmen. The days she works the early shift, she opens the store about 4:30 A.M., selling bait and coffee and shotgun shells to those headed to the Atchafalaya Swamp. Then, after the sportsmen give it up for the day, they compare notes and lies and gossip around a table in the back of the bait shop, boasting and joking in French. Jeanette sits primly behind the counter, the scout mother of a camouflaged troop of randy reprobates.

I have seen Jeanette arrive home, tired from waking up at 3 A.M. and working hard all day. Then she begins her domestic duties. She will cook a full supper for the entire extended family, which, quite often, to our great and good fortune, includes us. After supper a grandchild will wander in with a rip in her school uniform, and Jeanette, without complaint, will fix the garment before bedtime. Her house on any given day could be in a photo shoot for *Better Homes and Gardens.* Despite the constant parade of hunters, kids and in-laws, Jeanette keeps a perfect house and a calm demeanor. She is a natural wonder. For the Latiolais family, she is the tie that binds, the hand that feeds, cleans, and strokes fevered foreheads.

I once tried to make a list of our friends who have had the distinct privilege of eating a Cajun feast prepared and served by Jeanette. She insists on feeding our visitors, and they never forget the meal. No matter where else we take them to eat, guests go home raving about the hospitable Jeanette and her amazing and laden table. The long list of my friends who have put their swamp-muddied feet beneath Jeanette's table includes an airline pilot, an innkeeper, nurses, a dentist, a real estate broker, a lawyer, a home economist, reporters, a sister, an occasional cousin, niece, or nephew.

All of them at one time or another entered a kitchen full of fetching smells and fluffy rice and small children racing about and asking Jeanette for things. They left with new friends, old recipes, usually spoken not written. There's also an outside kitchen, where Johnelle keeps his big gumbo pots and decorative gourds and heirloom tools. For the intoxicating smells alone, they could charge admission to either Latiolais kitchen.

Whenever anyone says something demeaning about Cajuns, I immediately think of Jeanette, her selfless way of living, and how good she is to strangers. I get fighting mad. I don't think we've ever had out-of-town company that Jeanette didn't go all out for—with shrimp gumbo or smothered turtle or her trademark potato salad—a culinary *bienvenue* to a strange new land. I always hesitate to add to Jeanette's work load, but I end up depending on her the same as everyone else. People rely on her, and she delivers. Jeanette loves people, including us, and to be loved by Jeanette is a wonderful thing.

CAJUNS HAVE BEEN THE subject of scorn and ridicule for a lot longer than they've been celebrated as fun-loving free spirits. From the Anglos in charge of the local school systems when Jeanette was a girl, to the literature at the turn of the century, French Cajuns have, through the years, been portrayed as shiftless and ignorant. Until relatively recently, they have been made to feel ashamed of their culture, their language, and their ancestors. The battle for respectability has been long and not altogether successful.

So when I heard that Paris Hilton and her silly "reality" television show, *The Simple Life 2*, was filming an episode in Henderson, I shuddered. The whole premise of the dumb show was for the city princesses to mock and make fun of the simple lives they invaded. They parachute into some hick setting, make jokes at the expense of the host family, then head off down the highway in their princess-pink pickup and travel trailer. What a concept.

First we heard Paris was coming, which was perversely fascinating enough. I had only recently discovered Paris Hilton was not a French hotel. Then we heard that much of the filming would be at the marina where Don keeps his skiff, a beautiful landing that is home to a business called Houseboat Adventures. Paris and sidekick Nicole Richie ostensibly would be "staying" with a family we knew well, Mr. Doug's son and daughter-in-law, Mitch and Laurette Mequet. The city women would go crawfishing, frog-gigging, and shopping, of course, to help prepare Mitch and Laurette's teenaged daughter Jenny for her first date. I shuddered again.

We were in Henderson part of the time Paris and Nichole were there. My niece and nephew were spending their spring break with us in the swamp. There were Paris sightings, and one day the crew filmed Don and my nephew Scott coming in from a boat ride. That footage with my nephew Scott was cut, but Don's boat actually has a cameo in the forgettable episode.

Atchafalaya Swamp has been documented by outsiders countless times. Johnelle and Frank once fought over the binoculars to watch a Penthouse shoot on a houseboat near the old *Green Queen*'s marina. Ken Burns talked to swamp-dwellers for his excellent documentary on Huey Long. Props from Hallmark's movie *Old Man* and that big-screen dog, *Southern Comfort*, still float about in the swamp. The movie *Shy People* with Barbara Hershey was made in the area.

So Paris's pink pickup pulling an Airstream didn't really make much of a splash. Mitch and Laurette reported the "girls" had been polite and nice, and their son Jude proudly showed me his autographed photos of the skimpily clad stars. We pretty much forgot all about it till the episode was about to air and Scott reminded me to watch.

It could have been worse. The show went relatively easy on

the Cajun family and the swamp. *Simple Life* already had done hatchet jobs on rural families in Mississippi and Arkansas, and I anticipated the same treatment of the Cajuns. The result, I'll admit, wasn't as horrible as I had feared. In Cajun Country, the rich girls retracted their claws.

Theirs was, of course, a superficial snapshot of the culture with a contrived plot: shy Jenny gets fashion and dating pointers from the world-weary city women. The irony was that the Cajuns seemed more interesting and exotic than the traveling starlets. By being themselves, they spoiled the show's silly formula.

Except for Mr. Doug, everyone in Henderson seemed okay with the finished product, if they watched at all. Some did not bother. Mr. Doug took exception to the show's final comment, the one Paris made about his granddaughter. Paris and Nichole supervise Jenny's first date, and then congratulate themselves on how good the teen looked.

"She'll be pregnant in a year," Paris says, a gratuitous parting shot and totally in character for the ice princess.[7]

Not long after the show aired, I hired Jude, Jenny's brother, to give a friend and me a short swamp tour. I complimented him on his brief television career. Jude had taken Paris and Nicole on the televised frog-gigging trip. The magic of TV made it look like the rich visitors were catching the frogs all by themselves.

Don was in Mississippi and his skiff was dry-docked. So Jude obliged us with a quick tour, zooming about the Atchafalaya Basin with the confidence of the very young. Every now and again he would slow the boat enough to nod in the direction of a big bird, and say, "Blue heron." Or "Gray heron." Or "Egret." A man of few words, but then we weren't paying much.

Making conversation, my friend asked Jude if he had made plans for after high school. More to the point, she asked if he planned after graduation to leave the swamp. If he planned ever to leave the swamp.

"Why would I?" he asked, not missing a beat.

Back at the landing, without a word, he showed us an autographed photograph of himself standing with the scantily clad Paris Hilton and her skinny sidekick. Jude had a devilish grin on his face.

I thought about what he'd said about not leaving the swamp. Why would he? Why should he? The Outside World had come to him. And, to his delight, a couple of high-profile starlets had said they would love to come back.

Hollywood Might Need Cajun Louisiana, but Cajun Louisiana Doesn't Need Hollywood

Mary Lee Higginbotham searches for a cigarette in the velvety bottom of a Crown Royal bag. "I have a severed vocal cord, and still I smoke" she rasps in testimonial.

Mary Lee is an attractive slip of a woman in a denim jumpsuit. She is friendly as a veteran bartender, which she is. She has even fired barmaids who won't talk to the customers. It's not acceptable behavior. Mary Lee and her husband, Red, have owned Red's Levee Bar for nearly five decades. Situated across the levee from the swamp at Catahoula, it is a neat but modest establishment with hardwood floors, two pool tables and a cypress clock with the numeral "5" at every position. The clock's lettering says: "I never drink till 5."

Things are quiet. A couple of crawfish fishermen are having an early afternoon brew. If they were to down too many, it could get confusing. The garish sign painted in gold and red on the vinyl outside doesn't say Red's Levee Bar; it says "Texas Red's State Line Bar."

This isn't the state line, and it isn't Texas. And Mary Lee wants her storefront put back the way it was.

In September 1997, Robert Duvall and his movie crew used the bar and Mary Lee's house right next door while filming *The Apostle*. In the movie, Duvall is an evangelical preacher from Texas who hides in Louisiana after killing his wife's lover. While hiding, he starts a church. But first, while on the run, the Apostle sinks his car in a lake, then buys a bus ticket to Louisiana. Part of the sign at Mary Lee's that's not really Mary Lee's says "Bus Tickets Inside." In real life, there are no bus tickets inside.

"He was a real shy man," Mary Lee says of Duvall. "A great actor, but a shy man. He didn't say anything unless you talked to him first."

The movie shoot at Red's Levee Bar took about three days, and most of the footage from those three days bit the dust. Mary Lee hasn't seen the movie, but somebody told her Red made it in but her Chihuahua did not.

"This is my baby," she says of the trembling saucer-eyed dog beside her. "I didn't care about Red, but I wanted my dog in the movie."

It was a hectic business, hosting Hollywood. For a couple of days, Mary Lee couldn't even find her telephone. And the stars didn't shine so bright in person. Of Farrah Fawcett, who plays Duvall's wife, she says, "Makeup can do a whole lot for some women."

A lot of folks might thumbtack a movie poster on the barroom wall, leave the Texas Red's sign up as a curiosity, and play up the distinction of appearing in a much-discussed film. A lot of people might milk the moment. Not Mary Lee.

Mary Lee just wants things back the way they were—last September, and now it's March already—and she recently settled with the film company over the altered vinyl siding. She wants her original vinyl siding back, the heck with Hollywood.

"Somebody told me the movie didn't really have much of a story," Mary Lee says dismissively. "Nothing happens."

Staying Warm

The priest says the bride is known for her exuberant spirit, and that is true. The groom is a good man, and Father offers the new concrete walk outside the church as a handy illustration of just how he knows—the bridegroom built it.

This is a happy, humming season, a time when couples promise each other a better life. As it says in Ecclesiastes, ". . . how can one be warm alone?"

We make a special road trip from north Mississippi to Henderson: Mr. Doug is marrying again. After the death of his second wife, he met and courted Emmeline. She was a widow, living in her RV at a nearby RV park, a spunky kind of gal who drew Doug like a moth to a bug-zapper. She was by all accounts a *sport*, riding with him in an oversized dune buggy, accompanying him on faraway hunting trips, putting a smile on his once-sad face. She is also a wellspring of endearments: "Now *Punkin*," Emmeline will coax. She has the most theatrical way of speaking, as if the world really is her stage. "*Po' baby*," she'll lament, comforting people with anything from a sore throat to a hangover.

On a warm spring evening, at the little Henderson Catholic church, the two lovebirds in their sixties march down the aisle to a soloist's haunting rendition of "Amazing Grace." Bathed in forgiveness of candlelight, they vow to honor, obey, and cherish. And soon all of us leave the church for a reception that perfectly showcases the *joie de vivre* of French Louisiana. Life is a party; bring your own excuse. It's my first traditional Cajun wedding, and I love it. I have my favorite moments. At one point, as if everyone else hears a certain secret summoning bell, we all leave the reception hall to line up in the yard and the sweet night, behind the newlyweds. A wedding march—"La Marche des Maries"—cranks up and we slowly zigzag back inside and through the hall, in time with the amazing accordion and vocals, in a ceremony both solemn and serene.

It's the saddest, prettiest music I've ever heard.

The bride's mother, calm and happy, has been brought from her nursing home for the occasion. The bride's dog, a plumpish rat terrier called The Baby, wears a dress with a crinoline and preens for a dozen cameras.

The groom's cake reflects his love for classic cars, replete with icing fenders. The bridesmaids are a rainbow of sherbet colors. Everyone dances with everyone else, from babies to octogenarians, no lead feet here. Even I get a dance with the groom, who makes it look easy. They skip the traditional pinning of money on the groom's suit that I've read about, presumably because the couple is mature and established.

There is an innocence about the whole event, and I'm reminded of that wonderful Fitzgerald line in *The Great Gatsby*: "... they ... came for the party with a simplicity of heart that was its own ticket of admission."

DOUG AND EMMELINE WILL live in Henderson in an interesting home he has built on the edge of town. From the outside the house looks like a huge garage, a metal Butler Building affair with giant doors on one end. And it is three-quarters garage, where Mr. Doug will keep his classic car collection, his RV, and other toys. The apartment end is finished to a turn, with beautiful tile and custom cabinetry. You'd never guess looking at the building from the outside that such fine appointments are part of the inside. It is the design almost every man in America would prefer.

Mr. Doug used to say that when he retired he was moving from Lafayette to Henderson, where people take care of one another.

I understood what he meant. It's impossible to think about the families we know in Henderson without using that old, biblical verb "to cleave." Children don't so much leave home as they leave the house, often building another dwelling—or pulling in a mobile home—in the yard of one set of the parents. Many yards look like a diagrammed sentence on a grammar school chalkboard, with the dwellings of offspring "modifying" the old homeplace.

Jake Delhomme, the millionaire professional football star from Breaux Bridge, renovated his grandfather's former house, which, of course, sits chockablock to his parents' home on the Breaux Bridge Highway. A couple of Super Bowls later, he built a big, lavish home, also next door to his folks and just in front of the grandfather's house. Delhomme might have built a house anywhere, away from a busy, commercial road with a concrete truck headquarters and a dirt bike track. He wanted to stay close to his family. It was typical zoning for Cajuns.

Jeanette and Johnelle have two married sons, each with two children of their own. The sons' families live "in the yard," as Johnelle describes it, in double-wide homes. Johnelle's mother, Marjorie—everyone calls her Toot—has a trailer directly behind Johnelle's brick house, the better for Johnelle to take care of her. The scene always reminds me of the television show *Dallas*, where the many Ewings all lived on the same ranch, most of them in the same house, and gathered every afternoon at cocktail time to celebrate or to fight, whichever the occasion called for.

It is more than a physical closeness that binds Henderson families. There seems to be an accepted pattern of caring for their own that has disappeared from much of the rest of our country. The care follows loved ones into death. The cemeteries here with their above-ground vaults are fastidiously maintained, the tombs scrubbed personally and routinely by family members with bleach solutions to keep them gleaming and white.

I LOVE TO WALK through the cemeteries, which personalize the dearly departed in ways that reveal much even to strangers. Names are in the granite, of course, including nicknames. Then, often with engraved illustrations, the family tells you something about the dead person—a hand of cards illustrates she enjoyed playing the Cajun game *bourre*, a can of beer indicates he loved his beverages, a pirogue symbolizes his livelihood. Often on the tombs of teenagers you see elaborate engravings of the trucks or cars they died racing. What might be considered macabre or tasteless elsewhere is here loving tribute to lost loved ones. There are lots of photographs, too, of the dearly departed. All of the graves sit above the ground, same as in New Orleans, because the land is low and regularly floods.

Catahoula is home to my favorite area cemetery. Situated right next to beautiful Lake Catahoula, the small graveyard has monuments to fishing, hunting, card-playing, and shrimping. My friends Johnelle and Jeanette already have their names on two of the above-ground vaults.

Not long ago I went with my father to our two family cemeteries in our hometown of Colquitt, Georgia. He wanted to put Christmas flowers on family graves. We walked amongst the tombstones, reading names and dates and a few terse and saccharine engravings: Hope. Gone to Live With God. That kind of thing. I couldn't help but compare our Anglo-Saxon burial style with that of the Cajun French. We are more rigid and pompous—certainly in life, but even in death. I had firsthand knowledge of some of the dead we were walking amongst. Whiskey bottles, fishing boats, poker cards, and fast trucks would not have been out of place on a lot of the south Georgia graves, but there's a priggishness that inhibits such admission. Some might call it hypocrisy. In south Georgia you don't drive through an establishment and order up a daiquiri. You hide your moonshine in the trunk of a car. I'd wager the same amount of drinking, gambling, whoring, and lying go on in both places. Some are just better at hiding it.

That's one of the big differences in Cajun Country and the rest of the South, I think. There's a lot less hypocrisy here. The level of guilelessness is such that I'm not sure it ever occurs to the Cajuns that they should hide anything. When you're given cultural license to pass a good time and let the good times roll, what's to hide?

Angola Bound

I t begins with a prayer.

We are here, all of us—Jeanette and Johnelle, Don and myself—eager as virgins. As we watch, murderers, rapists, robbers, and assorted other convicted cowboys hold hands and form what's known in the evangelism business as a prayer circle. The preacher says a prayer that doesn't overlook anything.

"... Bless every head of livestock ..." the reverend beseeches.

That's how the Angola Prison Rodeo begins.

There'll be hollering, whooping, spills, a busted leg in the first ten minutes. But the spring version of the Angola Prison Rodeo begins with a purely Protestant prayer, a prayer to age an ACLU lawyer by a decade. If there's a Muslim or Jew or secular humanist among the five thousand in the Louisiana State Prison population, he doesn't speak up in protest today. Nobody wants to risk ending the rodeo.

And if there's a human emotion not triggered by the infamous Angola production, I don't know it. The annual fall rodeo (every weekend in October) became so popular with the public that one year they added a spring show. And this is the year we make it. Johnelle takes little convincing because he loves a day trip, especially if it involves ambulance sirens, food on a stick, and arts and crafts.

Angola is not in Cajun Country. Not technically. The drive

from Henderson takes about two hours, including a short ferry ride across the Mississippi River between the picturesque Louisiana towns of New Roads and St. Francisville. We jump out of the car as soon as the ferry gets underway, wanting to make the most of the experience. Johnelle stands silently by the railing looking regally toward the other shore. He might be a pharaoh on a barge, surveying his kingdom.

Everyone from Henderson eventually makes the Angola pilgrimage, either as a rodeo tourist, or as a family member visiting an inmate, or—in a few unfortunate instances—as a prisoner. On the ride to Angola, Jeanette and Johnelle tick off one-by-one the people from Henderson who are here now. It's a little like listing acquaintances you know living in New York on an airplane ride there. You figure you probably won't see them—after all, New York is a mighty big place—but it's important somehow to know someone there. And everyone does.

We ride through those front gates into eighteen thousand acres of lush Louisiana, and immediately feel the pain of the permanent residents. All the manicured drives and blueberry patches and white fencing in the world can't make you forget that two-thirds of the men here are lifers, and this pretty place is one they cannot leave. Ever. Somehow all the landscaping and elaborate flower beds make that realization worse. One of the crafts on display, in fact, is the inmate-constructed wooden hearse that is used in the funerals of the majority who die here.

The Angola prisoner population is mostly from cities, mostly black, all men convicted of serious violent crimes. Nearly half are in for homicide. More than three thousand are here for life, most of the rest are serving twenty years or more. So you come in with eyes wide open, knowing these are tough customers, violent and flinty hard. You just don't expect to find engaging, clean-cut looking fellows with good manners—and an abundance of talent.

The pre-rodeo crafts show begins the emotional avalanche. It makes you sad; all that talent behind razor wire, dickering through a fence over a price of a parrot painting, or a steamboat made of matchsticks. The trusties are free to sell their own art and mingle with the visitors. The others, however, are watching from beyond the fence, trying to make eye contact and a little spending money.

One trusty is selling a jewelry box artfully constructed of folded Camel cigarette packages, a beautiful little relic brewed from the remnants of risky behavior and shellac. If he doesn't sell it today, a New Orleans gallery will take it and price it at five hundred dollars.

There are paintings, many of them with religious themes. Jailhouse conversions never go out of style.

This year one fellow spattered a canvas with a barrage of color and called it simply, *Anger Management.*

There are hundreds of leather shoes, leather purses, leather hats, and enough belts to reach from Louisiana to London. I bought a few bottles of Guts and Glory hot sauce, a couple of hats that said "Angola Prison Rodeo," and four leather saddle key chains. Johnelle strikes up animated conversations with several of the convicts, lingering so long at one booth I suspect he might have run into one of the men on his Angola list. But, no, that's just Johnelle's natural exuberance. He makes friends faster than I can tie my shoe. .

At other rodeo craft shows I've bought two oil paintings, both by convicted murderers. The money for crafts goes into the prisoners' personal accounts and I like the thought of that. But, I also loved the paintings. Especially one of them. The convict-artist was a Shreveport native. His painting is of a sharecropper's cabin at night, under a full moon. Children are lingering outside, playing, but the adults are seen through the windows of the little house, already going about their nighttime rituals. The artist, Gilbert Greene, told me he had painted his childhood home. Every time I look at that painting—which is often because it hangs in my Henderson living room—I think of that man, who once was a child savoring for games and play every second of daylight and the time beyond.

It is sad to think that all this talent is being sponsored and honed just a little too late. If only Joe Blow from Bogalusa had learned to build a beautiful pirogue before he took up stealing cars. If only John Smith of Opelousas had taken up a paint brush before he took up a gun. If only Sam Boudreaux had taken up wood-carving before he took up wife-carving. If only, on and on.

Both the crafts show and rodeo are proof somehow that prisoners can find dignity and pride doing hard time. I'll admit to preferring the craft show part of the day, yet I always get chill bumps when the main show begins. The Angola Rough Riders—the only real cowboys in the show, trusties from the prison range crew—gallop into the arena to the *Rawhide* theme, and I want to cry. Something about the rousing music, the men sitting ramrod straight in the saddle, the faces etched with hard lives—it's poignant. Still human, these men are, after all, with so much dignity. They still have pride in their work.

Then, before you can recover from that impression, you see the frightened face of some city boy who volunteered to ride a horse bareback in an event called the "Buddy Pickup." It's clear he's never been near a horse before and hasn't a clue how to approach the beast. I want to cry again, this time for a different reason.

In this customized event, riders sprint toward a barrel where the "buddy" waits to jump on the same roused horse, a horse not wild about the first passenger, much less a second. Often as not, the couple tumbles together into the arena dust.

These are, after all, cowpokes who don't get to practice, but with nothing to lose and glory to gain. They are all volunteers, happy for the distraction, eager to be heroes instead of state-sponsored goats for at least one day.

The most crowd-pleasing event is one called "Convict Poker." The rodeo program describes it: "The idea is simple. Four inmates sit at a table in the middle of the rodeo arena playing a friendly game of poker. A bull is then released and provoked by the clowns, the sole purpose of which is to unseat the poker players. If he blinks he loses. The last man remaining seated is a winner. . ."

It doesn't take long for the "friendly game of poker" to go wild. The card table flies away. Inmates scatter. The crowd goes nuts.

The last event of the day, "Guts and Glory," is equally dangerous. A poker chip is tied between the horns of the meanest Brahman bull available. Convict cowboys wait in the ring for the bull to be turned loose. Each inmate does his best to get the bull to charge him, hoping to get close enough to grab the chit.

This day a pretend cowboy actually grabs the bull by the horns and rides facing its head a brief distance before being tossed away like a used Kleenex. That's the guts part. The crowd approves. He stumbles to his feet and tries again, this time, somehow, successfully removing the prize. The crowd roars. That's the glory.

Angola Warden Burl Cain maintains the rodeo has changed the prison morale and atmosphere, given prisoners something to look forward to, something to excel at, a way to earn money. Considering the security risk, he must be confident in his views. You wouldn't want to invite ten thousand outlanders into the hard-time prison for an event that prisoners weren't gung-ho about.

Of all the approaches to prisoner rehabilitation and reform, this must be the most innovative, if not the most successful. Hard-time criminals behaving themselves for the chance to be thrown from a bronco, stomped by a calf, kicked by a cow, or pitched into the Louisiana sky by the charging horns of a mad bull.

For a week after the trip to Angola, we can talk of little else. Each morning Johnelle demonstrates the convict poker game for the denizens of the M&M. He plays the part of the charging bull to perfection.

Knife Cocker of the Year

A lady named Alice wore a Woody Allen rain hat, neat slacks and a serious expression. I watched as she disembarked her truck with a license plate that had an air-brushed rooster and the words "Sport of Kings." Despite her intentness, she looked far more approachable than most of the men around the cockfighting arena who seemed to disappear into their caps and low, muttered conversations. Turned out Alice loved to talk about roosters, same as a master gardener enjoys describing her posies.

First of all, fighting roosters are misunderstood, the grandmotherly Alice said. She might have been defending a prodigal son or nephew. They're not mean at all, she insisted, except, of course, to other gamecocks.

"I have one rooster I take to the nursing home," she said. Alice's mother-in-law, who was in her nineties, and all the other nursing home residents loved that bird: Number Sixty. The roosters are called by their tag numbers.

"And, it is beautiful!" Alice finished in a voice of utter conviction.

There you have it. Even little old ladies in Louisiana nursing homes are perfectly okay with cockfights, which are about as hard to find around Cajun Country as bottled hot sauces.

When I met Alice, Louisiana and New Mexico were the

last states in our union where cockfighting was legal—not to mention highly organized. Then, with the threat of bird flu and an increasing howl of foul from animal rights groups, New Mexico banned the sport. Today, Louisiana, like the Cheese in the nursery rhyme, stands alone. Not for long. The 2007 Legislature took action, and the governor signed into law a measure that will phase out cockfighting—the so-called sport of kings—by August 2008. The season runs roughly from January to July at most stadiums. In July the roosters begin to molt, and the season conveniently ends.

Defenders of the anachronistic practice say that the new law will only send cockfighting underground—and probably not that far. The "stadiums" where the cockfights traditionally have been held may be replaced with floating, illegal sites, but many predict not much else will change.

I met Alice in Cecilia, about six miles from our Henderson house, at what was then a permanent cockfighting stadium. You can find them all about the area, but this was the one closest to us. It was located on Old Potato Shed Road in, aptly enough, a converted potato shed and cannery. It had enough bleachers to seat several hundred spectators, a concession area and forty holding "stalls" with six rooster pens each. The stalls looked like tick-tack-toe boards. The owner explained that he planned to add pool tables and video games for the youngsters. Kids, he said, sometimes grow bored with the rooster fights.

It was Alice who led me to the cockpit, its sand floor surrounded by waist-high Plexiglas. A cockfight is something like a three-ring circus, with one main pit where each fight begins. Flanking the main pit are two "drag" pits, where wounded or exhausted chickens are taken to lunge at one another until one or both are dead. The roosters wear tiny aluminum knives placed over their natural leg spurs. The urge to fight to the death is bred into them. A federal law bans interstate transport of game roosters, a backdoor-way to try and stop the fights. Breeding has been a national business. The transport ban hasn't stopped the fights—at least not in Louisiana.

THE CECILIA STADIUM, OFFICIALLY the Atchafalaya Game Club, had a printed schedule. During the season, fights are held on Wednesday and Saturday nights. Spectators and rooster owners bet on the individual fights, and the gambling, of course, is a big part of the fascination. The house makes its money off of a modest admission fee and the concessions.

Like most sports, cockfighting doesn't come cheap. If you have a good bloodline, a hundred dollars, and a skilled pit man, you too can start the long journey toward a $6,000 purse for "Gaff and Knife Cocker of the Year."

All of this was perfectly legal when I met Alice. She and other enthusiasts seemed eager to show me the ropes. Yet every now and then someone admonished, "No pictures." And I wasn't even holding a camera. Just because something's legal doesn't mean it's pretty.

Sure, the animal rights crowd has always objected. Even Louisiana has PETA chapters. Each year bills that would outlaw the fights were introduced in the state legislature and then killed quicker than over-matched roosters. There were three such bills the year I saw the Cecilia cockfight. But Alice and other passionate patrons over the decades have joined the Louisiana Game Bird Association and lobby against cockfighting opponents. Not until New Mexico opted out and left Louisiana the lone ranger did activists and image-conscious politicians join forces to get serious finally about stopping the blood sport. A first offense will call for a $1,000 fine and up to six months in jail. There will be, of course, an exemption for the chicken-chasing that goes on during the Courir de Mardi Gras (Mardi Gras Run) in several rural Acadiana areas. A lot of chickens die during those events, too. Masked horsemen ride from farm to farm begging for chickens and other gumbo ingredients. The chickens are tossed into the air, and the riders run to catch them. A chicken that's been a volleyball all day long might wish it were back in the pit.

Once I heard a matador intern in Spain defending the sport of bull-fighting. Those who object, she said, are guilty of cultural imperialism. It's something to think about. That said, most of the natives aren't wild about the sport that's synonymous with Spanish machismo. Finding a bullfighting fan in Spain has become as difficult as finding a Dutch person wearing wooden shoes.

In Louisiana, on the other hand, it's not that difficult to round up a room full of cockfighting enthusiasts. The Cajun culture is, after all, one that for centuries made its living by catching, trapping, skinning, gutting, filleting and using the natural world. One Cameron festival used to feature a rat-skinning contest and nutria toss. A PETA type must stay confused and overwhelmed by the challenges.

This might be the time for total disclosure. While cockfights are not my cup of tea—I don't like blood and I don't enjoy gambling—I have been to another cockfight, an illegal one. I wanted to write a column about it.

In 1986 a friend led me through the woods on an Alabama back road to a tin-topped stadium where fights had been hap-pening every other Saturday night since World War II. Inside the dusty, dimly-lit barn where roosters equipped with steel talons were tangling, it sounded for all the world like one con-tinuous corn flakes commercial. Men paid five dollars. Women got in free. At that time cockfighters paid forty dollars to enter a five-cock derby. The main pit was ground-level, surrounded with low, wooden sides. There were spectator bleachers, albeit rough and wood-hewn. There was a wood heater in the form of a fifty-gallon drum equipped with a flue for winter cockfights. There was a ladies' restroom, but the men went outside. The floors were dirt, packed hard from use.

One of the cardinal rules of the sport is this: Don't say anything bad about another man's rooster. Insult his wife, if you must, but not his rooster. The cock-fighter has not taught his bird to kill. Gamecocks are born knowing how. He has specially bred his bird and fed him high protein feed and "worked" him in various ways that strengthen rooster leg muscles. He has invested time, plus bought expensive gaffs. So bet against him, but don't say anything demeaning about his chicken.

THE FIGHT ITSELF HAS more technicalities than women's basketball. Terms like "Bill your roosters!" and "Handle!" mean something to the cocking fraternity. But to the uninitiated, a cockfight looks something like two men shaking feather dusters at each other.

When there's fresh poultry in the ring, the birds take an instant dislike to one another. Their long, straight hackles rise Tina Turner style. Sometimes a high-breaking bird jumps off the dirt floor and puts on a show; more often the birds shuffle close to the ground until the gaffs tangle or puncture some vital organ or other. The winner, basically, is the rooster left alive or the one pecking last.

It is not a particularly bloody blood sport. The sharp gaffs make tiny puncture wounds, not slashing cuts. In fact, it can be tedious. Many would find it appalling. It is not pleasant to watch blood bubbles foaming from a rooster's beak. You can rationalize, and many do, by remembering the chicken eaten every Sunday, the one shackled to a conveyor belt and stunned with an electrode before its head is cut off, guillotine-style. At least gamecocks die a natural death.

I wanted to ask Alice, but did not, what happens when Number Sixty meets its match. No more show-and-tell roosters at the nursing home, I suppose.

I had just about made my peace with cockfighting when the politicians decided it had to go. My father once worked for a chicken processing and distribution center, so I know intimately that chickens, for food or for fighting, don't have a lot to look forward to, period. My dainty maternal grandmother, who made stitches so neat and even by hand that you couldn't tell they weren't done by machine, at least once a week, usually on Sunday, went out into the back yard and wrung a chicken neck or two. In her role as a farmer's wife, it was as common and necessary as washing her hands.

Doesn't Travel Well

I am in Jeanerette in search of some 113-year-old French bread. That is, the recipe is 113 years old, not the actual bread.

A bakery was started at this site in 1884; it says so right in the red bricks. For the last seventy-five years, someone in the LeJeune family has run things, using the same bread recipe and brick ovens as the founders did.

LeJeune's Bakery anchors a corner on Main Street in Jeanerette, which, because it is home to one of the region's largest cane-processing mills, calls itself "Sugar City." I once spent a few minutes at the Jeanerette Museum, or "Le Beau Petit Musee." The museum director played a video for me and a couple of touring snowbirds, all of us wanting a crash course in sugar. For two centuries this part of Louisiana has been a vital part of the industry. I learned a few terms, and that all the cane you see eventually yields juice and a fibrous residue called "bagasse." The bagasse—it's hard not to laugh when you say the word—is burned to power the plant; the juice is boiled and concentrated to a thick syrup that eventually becomes raw sugar. During season, the sugar mill runs twenty-four hours a day, feeding on cane from heaped hampers that slowly waddle into Jeanerette.

Today I am more interested in sweet things to eat than the

process. LeJeune's is one of the oldest bakeries in a state full of them, and is regionally famous for its brick oven, crusty French loaves, and gingerbread cakes made with sugarcane molasses. A red light flashes, same as at T-Sue's, whenever there's hot bread available, which is most of the time.

"Do you have any bread left?" I holler into a cavernous, white kitchen just before the posted closing time. I meant to get here earlier, but travel is slow on Louisiana back roads in late November. Cane farmers are still hauling their harvest to the sugar mills, pulling large hammocks that wobble across both lanes. Roadsides are littered with cane that doesn't make it beneath low bridges. All of St. Martin and Iberia Parishes looks like an unfinished game of pick-up sticks. The cane still standing in the fields—the harvests are slightly staggered to avoid traffic jams at the mills—may be the prettiest crop I've ever seen, with the exception of French sunflowers. The graceful stalks sway with the slightest breeze, giving the impression that the flat, treeless fields are a fierce green ocean before a storm.

"Four loaves left," the friendly baker says, broad smile on his wizened face. "I'm selling those, then I'm going home." I buy half his remaining stock. I would have bought all four and helped him leave early, but this is not the kind of bread you can save. It's made without preservatives, and best when fresh.

Before I make it to the curb, I sample. The crust looks like a topographical map of the Rockies. The color is caramel. It's as warm as a sleeping puppy and as good as I'd heard it would be.

"Nothing like you'd buy in a grocery store deli," the baker had promised.

He was right. I consider myself something of a bread expert, not to be confused with a bread snob. For instance, I prefer plain old white loaf bread with tomato sandwiches. As my dear friend Annie Bates says, it makes for such a nice color combination. And, a purist, I like my hush puppies without too many secret ingredients. I once heard of a contestant in a national hush puppy cook-off who added radishes. Radishes! That should be illegal. Finally, as proof of my open mind and non-elitist tastes: The lowly, see-through hoe-cake my mother used to fry up with corn meal, water, and grease is hard to improve on.

But when it comes to bread, the French are the undisputed masters. They are the ones whose picture you find in the dictionary under "bread—staff of life." Ever since my first sojourn to France, I've been searching for a domestic substitute. Once you've cut the roof of your mouth with the sharp crust of real bread on a train ride from Toulouse, a substitute is the best you can hope for. French Louisiana has, by far and away, the best bread in this country.

Sitting curbside and cradling my warm loaf, I considered going back inside and cutting a deal involving UPS shipments of bread to Mississippi. I once heard of such an arrangement— a San Francisco man who paid for daily loaves to be flown from Paris, and he with a handy ration of sour dough bread available locally!

But good sense prevails, and I leave with my loaf and a half. Besides, if I could get bread this good every day, I'd weigh more than a brick oven. French bread is a lot like a Southern accent. It doesn't travel well.

NEITHER DOES JOHNELLE. TRAVEL well, that is. Several times we've invited Johnelle to ride to north Mississippi with us and spend time in Iuka at our other little house. He usually agrees. Jeanette more often than not is tied down by family obligations or her job, but Johnelle, for a few years now, has been reasonably free to travel. And, after I left the Atlanta newspaper, I had lots more time to play hostess.

If you've ever traveled with a child, you can envision the scene. By the time we leave Jackson, Mississippi, and hit the picturesque Natchez Trace, Johnelle is sick of riding. "How many hours do we have left?" he will ask. Then he slumps down into the passenger seat, fidgeting with his hands or perhaps munching loudly on a piece of hard candy and pouting. "How many miles is that?"

I'm going to brush with broad stroke here, but I feel fairly safe about it. Cajuns drive like bats out of hell. Every last one of them. As a result, the Natchez Trace with its sane, fifty-miles-per-hour speed limit is, to them, like standing still. Johnelle hates traveling the Trace. He is not the Lone Ranger. Doug Mequet, who traveled it once to visit us, calls it "that pretty road" with as much disgust in his voice as if he were saying "that miserable wagon trail full of potholes."

"There has to be another way to get here besides that purty road. I'm going back the interstate," Doug declared. "That purty road is too slow."

Once we finally make it to Iuka with our Cajun cargo, Johnelle is fine. For about two days. On the first day of his visit, we phone up all of the friends Johnelle's made in our little town. He has lots more friends in Iuka than we do. People here adore him. They should. Whenever anyone from Iuka visits Henderson, Johnelle cooks for them, gives them fishing and hunting tips, provides directions to various restaurants and bars, sends them home with souvenirs and memories and big aluminum pots in which to make a gumbo. So whenever word leaks out—usually via Johnelle's cell phone—that our Cajun visitor has hit town, eager men and women converge on our little farmhouse, eager to show Johnelle that Louisiana doesn't have a complete monopoly on passing a good time. Everyone from the tee-totaling local veterinarian to our rowdy lake friends come by to pay homage to Johnelle.

On the second day of his visit, we have an official party. One year, when Jeanette was free to make the trip, too, the couple brought two dozen pounds of crawfish and cooked étoufée for the crowd. Whatever the menu, Johnelle paces the floor until the first guests arrive. It's never soon enough for him. A typical Cajun party begins early in the day and lasts long into the night. As soon as the first pickup roars up the driveway, Johnelle is "on." He laughs, eats, smokes, and basically has a ball partying down with the diverse group he calls "the hillbillies."

ON THE NEXT DAY, the third day, the official party behind us, Johnelle's ready to return to Henderson. He's been gone too long. His family needs him. He misses Jeanette's cooking. Though the eight hours between the two towns is a long trip for what has amounted to a two-day vacation, we always try to oblige. A homesick Johnelle is not a fun Johnelle.

Once, however, Johnelle made the mistake of visiting in January. On the day Don was set to return him to Henderson, it snowed. The temperature only reached zero. Nobody was going anywhere. Johnelle, in his flimsy, nylon, temperate-weather coat and no hat, periodically tried to stand outside to smoke as Jeanette had told him he must. I insisted he could smoke wherever he wanted, inside or out. We would risk the second-hand smoke danger during such frigid weather. He courteously went outside anyhow, where he was the picture of misery, a shivering soul taking long drags and longing for home.

Johnelle, on that third day, began to pace and cuss and complain and otherwise fill the bill for Benjamin Franklin's description of guests who stay too long. I tried to cook interesting meals, but I'm no cook under normal circumstances. And Johnelle was in a foul mood, unwilling to cut me any slack. He started phoning Jeanette each day about suppertime, then reciting lovingly the menu that he might be having if only he'd had the good sense to stay at home. "She's smothering a roast, and cooking white beans," he'd say with a meaningful sideways look at me. I was knocking myself out to find and cook acceptable fare, but Johnelle wasn't buying it.

Because the Cajuns we know well are so content at home, the corollary is true. Like the wonderful French bread made in brick ovens, they only last about a day on the road. Even distances seem longer in their minds, another sign of a contented breed. If you don't travel much, a hundred miles seems more like a thousand.

Once, trying to make conversation while getting my hair cut in a Lafayette salon, I asked the cute young stylist if she were from the area. Listening to her heavy Cajun accent, I assumed she was.

"Oh, no!" she said, acting almost offended, as if I'd asked if she'd had enhancement surgery. "I'm from St. Martinville, me."

That's about ten miles away.

Courir de Mardi Gras

One long ago summer, trolling for columns, I pointed my Ford west. That's the way I managed to find four columns a week for so long, the sum of my logistics. I'd simply get in the car with an open mind, half an idea, or maybe two, and enough clothes to last about a week. Then I'd drive. And drive some more. This was long before cars came equipped with those gee-whiz, geo-positioning systems; I simply glued a dime-store compass to the dashboard. It's amazing how many times over the years it helped to know the general direction I was headed. This time it was Custer battlefield. If a columnist can't wax philosophical about a Last Stand, she should hang up her guns.

Fate is sometimes kind to desperate columnists, which, of course, is a redundancy; any writer with four deadlines a week is desperate. It was dumb luck, but I happened to drive near Sturgis, South Dakota, during the annual Harley-Davidson motorcycle rally. That infamous gathering transforms a sleepy cowboy town into a rowdy metropolis of jubilant Hog riders. A couple of hundred miles out from Sturgis, motorcycles began showing up along the highway, swarms of them, thick as mosquitoes in the Atchafalaya. At first I thought it was mere happenstance—and that road-running appeal the West has the rest of the country is lacking: no speed limits.

All the bikers greeted one another with a simple question

shouted over the roar of their machines: "You coming or going?" I heard it at fuel and tourist stops, restaurants and honky-tonks. "Coming or going?" I couldn't figure what on earth they were talking about. Were they talking about the Pacific Ocean? Was there some super mechanic west of the Rockies? After someone finally explained to me about the rally, I simply had to get to Sturgis. I was going.

I pulled in around noon. The town was so crowded I did something I rarely ever do. I decided to worry a few hours ahead of dark about a place to sleep that night. I knocked on doors and drove up pig trails where strangers said there might be lodging. All the motels, bed and breakfasts, camping areas, and parking lots were full, and private residences that rented rooms for the week already were booked, had been booked, most of them, for months. There was nothing, no room at the inn, no bunk at the bunkhouse, for a fifty-mile radius or more. The only other time I got bitten by my no-reservation habit was in Alaska, and then, at least, I was able to rent a converted container car for the night. Even without a bathroom, that was an acceptable, even fun, situation.

I wasted most of that day searching for a place to lay my head, until finally, around 10 P.M., I ended up back in downtown Sturgis in a parking lot. I decided there was nothing to do but spend the night in my truck. My aforementioned head ended up on a pillowcase full of dirty clothes, and my feet were curled in a contortionist's pose in the passenger seat.

All night long I nervously waited to be knifed, raped, or otherwise molested. The bikers I'd talked to were amazingly normal, even professional, folks—pediatricians from St. Louis, grandparents from Peoria, newlyweds from Maine. I didn't talk to a single Hell's Angel type; the bikers were almost disappointingly tame. But the local newspaper was full of rally-related headlines, including a couple of murders. Somewhere abroad was the tough and tattooed underbelly of this fraternity; I simply hadn't seen it yet. I have never been afraid of traveling alone; in fact, in a lot of ways I prefer it. Especially when you're working, there's an advantage to having only your own needs to consider. This was a little different, camping in an unlit parking lot. It was simultaneously exciting and scary. For hours I could hear the vroom-vroom of bikers as they cranked off into darkness. I guess I slept a little. At dawn the next day I sleepily drove away with melodramatic glee, grateful to be alive.

That was Sturgis.

THE SECOND LARGEST CONVERGENCE of Harley riders I've ever seen was in an even more unlikely place, little Mamou in Evangeline Parish, a Cajun prairie town northwest of Henderson near Opelousas. On normal days Mamou is a quiet town of about thirty-five hundred, tidy as a school marm. On Fat Tuesday, it is transformed.

I had read a good bit about the peculiarly Cajun Courir de Mardi Gras—the running of the Mardi Gras—and wanted to see one. There are several in the prairie towns of Acadiana. Turns out, every biker in the Southeast also had a yen to see the Mardi Gras Run.

Never is the cultural confusion over what's bona fide Cajun and what's not as heightened as when you're talking Mardi Gras. The larger towns, Lafayette and New Iberia, and even some of the smaller ones, including Henderson and St. Martinville, have adopted the New Orleans-style Mardi Gras parades. The crowd comes near or at the appointed parade time and both parade participants and spectators ape what they have seen in the Big Easy or on television. Bands march and floats roll. Krewe members ride atop the extravagant floats and throw beads, doubloons, and plastic cups to the cheering, jostling crowd.

"Throw me something, mister."

It's amazing how your competitive nature will out during a Mardi Gras parade situation. Grown women will elbow children out of the way to catch plastic beads or cups. People bedecked like Christmas trees stumble home with the booty.

Lafayette, the area's big city, has several parades on and leading up to the big day. We had attended a few typical smaller parades, in St. Martinville and in New Iberia, where, quite by accident, I stood on the street right next to the mayor. We benefited from this lucky bit of geography. A lot of the good beads—read that, large—were thrown in our general direction by various brown-nosers trying to hit their boss. It had rained a gully-washer earlier that day in New Iberia, such an impressive downpour that for a time I was doubtful Mardi Gras would roll.

"Any hope that the Mardi Gras parade will still happen?" I asked a shopkeeper.

We both looked out at the steely skies and the dripping trees and Water World sidewalks. She cocked her head in a confident way and replied: "Not much can stop a Mardi Gras." For the millionth time in my life, I wished I could needlepoint.

A FEW OF THE prairie towns north of Interstate 10—fortunately and stubbornly—have stuck with the more traditional Cajun Mardi Gras, which doesn't follow the New Orleans pattern at all. The Mardi Gras Run is more like trick or treat on horseback, with a few dozen participants going from house to house, ostensibly to beg ingredients for a gumbo. In return, the residents are teased, serenaded, and entertained in their own country yards.

The riders are called, same as the day itself, "the Mardi Gras"—individually and as a group. All day long, from first light till dusk, the Mardi Gras perform dances, sing traditional songs, play pranks, chase chickens, climb onto rooftops and into trees, "kidnap" babies and otherwise torment the scattered rural homeowners who, in turn, give them bags of onions, peppers, rice, and, the ultimate prize, live chickens. The Mardi Gras wear homemade and sometimes ancestral wire masks with the rest of their kaleidoscopic costumes. They look like a cross between Ringling Brothers clowns and the Ku Klux Klan, as many of the colorful hats are pointed.

The Mardi Gras Run is organized and traditional and it, too, varies slightly from town to town. You might say it is a moving pageant. There is nothing remotely like it anywhere else. For each Mardi Gras there is a captain, called *le capitaine*, and usually a co-*capitaine* or two. The leaders wear no masks, the better to do their job as liaisons between the hopped-up and wild Mardi Gras and the spectators. Someone, after all, must say when it's time to move along. A typical Mardi Gras will make thirty or forty stops during the day, and there are a lot of miles between begging stops.

The number of spectators keeps growing every year. With the current popularity of everything Cajun, there are now even wagons for hire that follow the Mardi Gras and their horses through the countryside, allowing tourists to witness the ritual that used to be seen only one household at a time.

All Fat Tuesday the Mardi Gras rides through countryside flat as a kitchen table. A couple of towns, Tee Mamou (Little Mamou) and Basile, have abandoned horses and replaced them with truck-drawn wagons in an effort to cover more territory quickly. But the game is ultimately the same. At the end of the day, the Mardi Gras ends up back in the center of town where most of the spectators wait. An expectant crowd gathers to watched the exhausted, sometimes drunken Mardi Gras parade down Main Street, riding their horses backwards, performing daring stunts and holding high their by-now dead chickens. Afterwards, the Mardi Gras grab a quick nap before the night's gumbo supper and an all-important dance, the Mardi Gras ball.

I wanted to see. Who wouldn't? There are so few true cultural oddities left in our world. So one warm February day, Don, Johnelle, and I loaded up for Mamou, which has a reputation for a really raucous parade at day's end. Jeanette was working and unable to go with us. We arrived early afternoon, and the scene was that of any small-town street festival. A band was playing, an artist was painting children's faces, and a lively assortment of people was milling around the street eating funnel cakes and corn dogs. Hundreds of Harley riders strutted about in their leathers waiting, like everyone else, for the Mardi Gras riders to return. One woman wore a dress made entirely out of purple velvet Crown Royal bags; I had never realized how appropriate the regal little bags are for Mardi Gras, replete with their gold lettering. Mostly, though, spectator attire was subdued and rather unspectacular, nothing like the New Orleans scene. Only a few wore costumes. The Harley riders made spectacular entrances, checked out one another, but soon began to look bored.

As DUSK NEARED AND I began to wonder if the trip had been worth the effort, the streets came alive. Excitement grew and someone yelled out, "They're coming! They're coming!"

Like a shooting star or a fabulous fireworks finale, the parade that wasn't really a parade was short, but amazing while it lasted. Exhausted riders, maybe two dozen of them, somehow found their second wind for the triumphant ride through town. I thought of King Arthur's knights, returning victorious from some battle, wearing all their war gear and showing off for the ladies. This was something like that. Masked men did tricks on their mounts that Mary Lou Retton wouldn't have attempted on a pommel horse. Often they fell. Some of their costumes were covered with Louisiana mud. There was none of the rhythmic, lazy strutting of the New Orleans' parades, no marching band. This was more thundering hooves and war yelps and the twirling of dead chickens.

The Mardi Gras, meaning the riders themselves, actually displayed an admirable indifference to those of us lining the street. Nobody threw beads or even paid much attention to lowly spectators who had waited half a day for this climax. It was a great show, but those of us on the street were as incidental as leaves banked in the gutters. You got the feeling the best part of Mamou's Mardi Gras was over—or yet to come. We were privy to only a tiny sliver of the live theater, watching hung-over men on their way to a nap necessary before they had the energy to enjoy the rest of a private adventure.

There are complaints from Cajun scholars and purists about the *courir de Mardi Gras* being corrupted by its increasing popularity with outlanders. They especially object to the tourists who pay to ride along in wagons and thereby feel entitled to participate in a celebration they don't really understand. They aren't even wild about the in-town bystanders, including myself, who don't know what to expect and are from outside the little host communities. Johnelle, who had never witnessed a Mardi Gras run, seemed just as extraneous as Don and I. We all were crashing a private party.

Cajun Mardi Gras is rite of passage for young Cajun males, not to mention a prelude to Lent. It's all about communities and neighbors, about knowing well the person behind the wire mask despite the fact you can't recognize him this one special day.

THE HARLEY RIDERS, IN particular, just didn't seem to fit into the formula of horses, rural rituals, and the big pot of gumbo at the rainbow's end. They looked a lot more natural in Sturgis, swelling the local population, true, but being the center of attention, not bystanders on bikes. You don't ride a Harley to be part of the audience.

I enjoyed the scene, but I will not go again. That day I got the distinct feeling that you really must be a rider or a resident or a gumbo cook or a mask-maker to enjoy the celebration's full benefit. The fun is in the continuum—handmade masks handed down from generation to generation, century-old French songs sung at every stop along the day's route, the honor of being captain, the mystery of dressing in costume.

The parade part was over quickly. The incongruous Harleys roared off into the horizon and the next street festival. We loaded up for the hour's ride back to Henderson. Once again, I had that funny feeling of not really belonging. There was no real role for me in Cajun Mardi Gras, not even the one of saying, "Throw me something, mister!" I could stand on the sidelines and send up a cheer, but the parade would go on with or without me. In that festive crowd in the Cajun prairie, I felt a little lonely.

One of my favorite novels is Frederick Exley's *A Fan's Notes*, the first installment of his partly autobiographical, partly fictional trilogy. The book takes its name from the author's early epiphany experienced while he is watching his professional football hero play heroic football. He suddenly realizes he is destined to sit in the stands and cheer, nothing more. He is a fan, not a gridiron hero. It is perhaps the saddest moment of youth, the day you realize you are many things, but mostly you are ordinary. More or less the same as everyone else.

I think fighting that reality, the common curse of being ordinary, is why people buy Harleys, or join Mardi Gras krewes. It is why we all enjoy frivolous festivals and extravaganzas and wearing exotic masks, whatever the excuse. It is why some dye their hair blond, or purple, or run marathons, or go back to school after mid-life. We are saying to ourselves and to anyone else who bothers to notice, "I'm different, not ordinary at all. I'm a wolf in sheep's clothing, don't cross me. I'm wild, untamed, apart from the pack."

I know damn well it's why people write books.

You could break your neck going to Louisiana festivals. The state publishes a fat directory of festivals each year, including, in our region, the Duck Festival in Gueydan, the Frog Festival in Rayne, the Crawfish Festival in Breaux Bridge, and the Bastille Day celebration in Kaplan.

The first festival of the year every year, and one of the most unusual, is the Louisiana Fur and Wildlife Festival in Cameron each January. In 2005 Hurricane Rita laid waste to most of Cameron, hurtling much of its population elsewhere, including one family to our street in Henderson. But in 1999, when I made it to the Fur Festival, it was a wild and jubilant time.

Don and I spent the night before in a shack of a motel room on nearby Holly Beach. The weather was frigid—perfect for a Fur Festival—and the only heat came from gas burners on a diminutive stove. The window panes rattled all night from a cold wind off the Gulf. You had to get up extra early in the morning to make the National Ladies' and Men's Muskrat and Nutria Skinning competition, and I meant to. But the wind was howling, I'd finally found a warm spot in bed, plus I'm always a bit squeamish about watching live things get skinned. We didn't get to Cameron until just before last year's Fur Queen, Summer Leigh, floated down main street behind a school band. It was probably our loss. I read later in a Fur Festival scrapbook that one champion twenty-something years ago skinned five muskrats in fifty-two seconds. Talk about your fur flying.

The scene was about as politically incorrect as any I've seen the last two decades. Women wore their fur pieces—it was cold as the Tundra—and children their Davy Crockett coonskin hats. Most of the town's male population had on camouflage hunting garb, not unlike the Henderson uniform. Kids walked by carrying guns for the trap-shooting contest.

We actually happened upon the frigid festival by accident. We'd been exploring the virtual isolation of the Gulf Coast Marsh and stopped at a store for gas. The clerk asked if we were on our way to the Fur Festival. "What Fur Festival?" I asked. Then she rhapsodized about the various contests for oyster-shucking and duck-calling and the retriever dog trials. Used to, she said, they'd hurl a duck into the marsh with a giant slingshot for the retriever trials.

Next thing we knew, we were standing on a crowded side-walk, fighting for Fur Festival doubloons and watching floats that celebrated wildlife and the petroleum industry all in one bundle of bunting. There was gumbo, shrimp on a stick, and hundreds of other ways to add calories to keep you warm during January on the Louisiana coast.

Old Trash Pile Road

When we first began our house hunt, Don was fascinated by a lane off of Main Street in Henderson with the descriptive name of Old Trash Pile Road. "Just imagine," he said. "If we had that address, we'd never again get a credit card come-on."

There's a bit of the reverse snob in both of us, and in a pretentious world of fancy subdivisions sprouting in former cow pastures and cane fields, we loved the honesty of the name. Too many times developers assign exotic, ill-fitting monikers to places that are ordinary or worse. Old Trash Pile Road seemed both direct and desirable. I guess we'd seen too many Hilltop Terraces where there were no hills or terraces, or Halcyon Estates where there was no peace.

We went so far as to take a couple of long rides and lackadaisical looks for a house or a lot on Old Trash Pile Road, but nothing was for sale. We bought our place on Dupuis Street and forgot all about it. Until one day in passing when Don noticed that the Old Trash Pile Road sign had been replaced. It now said Romaine Robin Road. We asked Johnelle and Jeanette about the change.

"The other children were making fun of kids who lived on Old Trash Pile Road," Johnelle explained. "They changed it." Whenever school forms were filled out, or addresses mentioned aloud, the kids from Old Trash Pile were given a hard time. They were trash from an old trash pile, ha ha. Evidently, even in a town with a boy baker named Sue, that harassment wouldn't do, not in today's world that believes above all else in nourishing youthful self-esteem.

I thought about it. In one respect, it was probably a wise thing to change the road's name rather than have even one child hang his head. I know all about how cruel the younger set can be. I had watched in the Tool Shed Reading Club, for instance, as the kids tormented one another over things as silly as the color of shoe laces or the inability to ride a bicycle no-hands for an entire block.

On the other hand, how much better life would be if we all, at any age, could be a little more honest with ourselves, if we could call things the way we see them. I've worked for a newspaper so politically correct you dared not use the word "black"—as in "black" day or "black" mood—for fear of offending black staff members. Writers have feelings, too. And we need all the words available for trying to write clearly, succinctly, and descriptively. As with the poet's advice to use "an empty doorway and a maple leaf" to evoke "all the history of grief," somehow naming a road for an old trash pile was an exercise in graphic purity.

ANYHOW, A SINGLE TRASH pile—we never actually saw one on the road—would have been a vast improvement over the helter-skelter litter that pocks most of our parish. If, truly, the trash had been limited to one big pile on a wooded road, that would make at least some kind of sense. Especially since there is no official landfill in the entire parish. The nearest official dump is a private one in the neighboring parish of Iberia.

The accepted way of getting rid of old refrigerators, bed-steads, sofas, tires, bicycles, potted plants, mattresses, car parts, boats, engines, air conditioners, and other sundry refuse is to drive to the levee and dump it when nobody's looking. I'm not sure it would make that much difference if someone were looking.

Thumbing through a magazine one day, I saw a cute idea for a flowerbed. The featured gardener had plugged an old iron bedstead into the ground and used landscape timbers to outline the rest of his "bed." A colorful quilt of flowers was planted inside. Soon as I saw the picture, I wanted to copy. Without passing go, I loaded up in our truck and cruised the levee until I found an old metal headboard. It took about five minutes. There were plenty to choose from. I had my choice of colors. That's how bad the dumping problem is along the levee.

The worst dump sites along the levee are about ten minutes away from the Disney World of rest stops, an extravagant, overwrought, state-of-the-art complex that uses an animated alligator to entice tourists into a dark room where an upbeat movie shows them the many charms of the Atchafalaya. Before this rest stop, there was another, perfectly adequate one on the same site. They tore it down and built the lavish new one. The carefully edited film they show never once pans a floating dog carcass or a refrigerator rusting on the bank.

The amazing natural world that state tourism tries so hard to sell is daily fouled by the inhabitants. And neither state nor local government bothers to provide an alternative dumping site or sees a contradiction. Louisiana invites the world to come and enjoy the natural bounty, but makes no effort to keep itself clean.

I have a real problem with litter and litterbugs. Since the days of television's anti-litter, crying Indian—I once met the actor who was the crying Indian, at Mississippi's Choctaw reservation—I've had little patience with that crime against nature. You would think we'd be beyond tossing our trash out of car windows. But, no, not in the states where I live and have lived. Citizens are more worried about keeping the interior of their Corvettes and Camaros clean than they are about the landscape.

In so many charming ways, Cajun Country is fifty years behind the times. People speak to one another on the street. Men are chivalrous and children say, "Yes, m'am" and "No, sir." Adults, even those older than you, call you Miss Rheta and Mr. Don if they don't know you well. Clerks try to help you find things in stores. But I'm sorry to say Acadiana is fifty years behind in environmental concerns as well.

In Henderson, I spend half my time picking up the litter on our own street, beer cans and paper plates and fireworks paper that's spilled from trash cans that rarely ever leave the curb. There is a town ordinance—rare in that Henderson has few ordinances and those are seldom enforced—that says trash cans can only stay curbside 12 hours before and after the weekly trash pickup. Everyone ignores it. The police chief lives on our street, and the mayor lives about a block away. Yet half the neighborhood fails to collect its cans. Garbage day in Henderson—and the next day, and the next—is spent dodging cans with your automobile. They roll about the roads until some unlucky motorist creams one.

I find myself waiting until some of the neighbors roar off to work in their new extended-cab pickups. Then, like a thief, I rush into the street and tidy up after the garbage men. I wouldn't want to offend my neighbors by having them witness my fastidiousness. At times, amused at my own stealth, I think: "What's wrong with this picture?" Why am I suddenly self-conscious about picking up litter in front of my own house? You'd think I was aiming binoculars at a neighbor's house.

I DON'T WANT TO tar with too broad a stroke. Some of the houses in Henderson are the best-kept homes I've ever seen anywhere. Not only are some of the lawns kept fanatically neat, there are artful touches in gardening and grooming. One sweet lady has a meticulously maintained yard with a hand-lettered sign above it all saying: GOD ANSWERS KNEE-MAIL. But the perfectly neat places are often right next store to homes with muddy yards full of rooster huts, lumber piles, and oil drums. There seems to be an unwritten rule of laissez-faire landscaping. You tend to your business, I'll mind mine. No neighborhood covenants in Henderson, that's for sure. The town once had a zoning ordinance but people complained until they rescinded it.

Indifference to the general environment is slowly beginning to change. I recently read of a nonprofit group, the Save Our Cypress Coalition, that targets some of the nation's big box stores and asks them to cease sales of cypress mulch products. Louisiana's endangered cypress-tupelo swamps are regularly clear-cut to feed the mulch demand. Cypress forests—the few left standing—protected the rest of the ecosystem during Hurricane Katrina, and the cypress mulch has no real advantage over pine straw or pine bark nuggets, the group claims.

To be honest, there are a few other things in Henderson besides litter that I just don't get. Spoiling the natural beauty is at the top of my list, but I have other concerns. There's a terrible drug problem, especially among the juveniles. Seems like every trip to Henderson we hear of another teenager who is in rehab; the drug culture wouldn't seem to fit with the rural and sporting world that is Henderson, but it's there. I also don't get the fascination with speed. Even the youngest of children here have four-wheelers or dirt bikes. They roar about the cane fields and the back streets with abandon, tiny tots at the wheel. Children often bypass tricycles and Big Wheels and bicycles altogether and go straight for the motorized stuff. I don't understand that need for speed.

In the swamp you have your ear-busting air boats and bass boats. Sitting on a wharf at any of the local landings is peaceful only for a matter of minutes before some loud, exhaust-spewing contraption tears by. On land you have the largest pickup trucks I've ever seen collected anywhere on earth, and that means something considering my other home is in rural north Mississippi. With a couple of exceptions in my youth, I've never cared much what kind of vehicle I drove as long as it cranked when I turned the key. In Henderson, you are known by your ride. The bigger and fancier the better. "Well," said Don, defending that particular local priority, "you can live in your car, but you can't drive your house."

Not unlike north Mississippi, even the smallest towns have several auto parts stores, garages, and car washes. You might have to drive ten miles to find a library, but you can get your carburetor overhauled or your truck detailed a block away.

So near the vast natural expanse of swamp, it seems unlikely that people would care so much about the automobile. Nevertheless, they do. Likewise, and I admit to generalizing, there's a love for any other high-tech gadget that comes down the pike—or bayou, as the case may be. I first thought there might be a rare outbreak of ear-aches in the town; everyone you saw had a hand cupped around his ear. Then I realized that nobody who was anybody went anywhere without a cell phone. And Cajuns constantly use them. There is absolutely no cell phone etiquette here, and the young Vietnamese priest at the Henderson church finally had to lay down the law about the disruptive ringing during mass. That angered some of the parishioners.

I VACILLATE BETWEEN WANTING to complain to someone—about the free-floating garbage cans, for instance, which have annoyed me for ten years—and thinking I have absolutely no right. I've always hated Northerners who came South and spent their time telling us natives how they do things in Minnesota or Connecticut. I sure didn't want to stand up in some civic meeting with my weird accent—yes, I'm the one with the strange accent when in Henderson—and presume to tell the town fathers their business. After all, we only spend a few months out of the year here. As a reporter I've sat through too many long city meetings made longer by some prissy person just off the boat who objected to the local mores. I don't want to be that person.

One day my teenaged neighbor rudely warned me that his pit bulls would surely destroy the rug I was airing on the low, hurricane cross fence between our yards. I thought I had a ready retort. "Maybe you shouldn't keep such vicious dogs," I said.

"And maybe you ought to move somewhere else," he barked.

The old Love It Or Leave It bumper stickers from the 1960s immediately came to mind. That, in essence, is what the lad was telling me. Or, if you can't get with the program, as my father used to say, get out. We solved the pit bull problem by building a higher fence, a solid wood fence, a fence to make better neighbors. That seems to be the solution many in town choose. I would love to own a fence concession in St. Martin Parish. High fences lend themselves to the dramatically mixed neighborhoods. High fences aid the blind eye residents turn to a neighbor's nasty habits.

But the young man's words still ring in my ears whenever I dare to think any critical thoughts of this, my second home, my Oz. Maybe I ought to move somewhere else if I can't manage to adhere to the basic Cajun tenet, to live and let live. I think it's philosophical justice, really, considering the many times I've ranted against snooty subdivision covenants that decree that you can't park a pickup truck in front of your house, or that garbage cans must all be the same color and kept in certain out-of-sight locations. Some even bar utility sheds, which would mean no Tool Shed Reading Clubs anywhere. My complaints, really, are few compared to the many things I love about Henderson.

So I do not leave. I love.

I certainly do not march into a town meeting and demand changes and act like a fussy city woman. I mutter under my breath and continue to pick up trash on the sly and keep to myself a loathing of the few Cajun ways my Cracker heart cannot condone or understand.

Rue de Putt-Putt

Tony Latiolais is a wiry, timber hitch knot of a man who builds boats, old-style wooden pirogues and bateaus. He lives on a street in Henderson called Rue de Putt-Putt, named for the sound a bateau makes with its two-horsepower engine.

Tony grew up at the edge of the swamp, one of eight boys and four girls, a regular disciples' complement of children. His father taught his brother Albert how to make boats, and Albert taught Tony. If he were a cook, you'd say he starts from scratch. He builds boats from the old cypress logs brought up from the river or lake bottom, logs buried beneath water and muck for decades—Lazarus logs, commonly called "sinkers."

"The only ones I use were cut before 1930," Tony says between chain puffs on the cigarette that balances permanently, naturally, on his lip, like a freckle on a boy's nose. "The ones they're cutting now are too young, no good."

I have a weakness for both boats and purists of any sort. And a purist is what Latiolais obviously is. We talk in a carport/shop outside a house that Tony is building. He calls it his "bachelor pad," and the emerging cabin does have a rugged, pilothouse kind of appeal. It sits at the very end of the short street, just off of Henderson's main drag. The whole length of the lane seems to be populated with Latiolais brothers.

Any boat Tony builds begins with that swamp search for the right log, then its retrieval; construction doesn't get any simpler from there. The minimum cost of one of Tony's cypress pirogues is about $1,500, which barely covers his time. Few are willing or able to afford that much for a hunting boat— not when you can buy an aluminum or plywood pirogue for a fraction of the price. So, these days, Tony mostly fills custom orders, or builds boats for himself or Hollywood.

You might have seen Tony in a bit part in the Hallmark Hall of Fame movie *Old Man*, based on a Faulkner story. Tony's brother Dado Latiolais had a meaty role as the loquacious Cajun on a houseboat who befriends a prisoner and his female companion. Tony built the boat used in the movie, an old-fashioned bateau. He also built the wooden altar for a church scene in the Robert Duvall movie, *The Apostle*.

Tony's pride and joy is a boat he built in 1998 called a "putt-putt bateau," a style that evolved from the Cajun "chalon." The chalon was a motorless boat with flat bottom and raked bow and stern. Tony's is twenty-five feet long and equipped with a two-horsepower engine, but some traditionally had engines as powerful as eight horsepower. The putt-putts were the first motorized boats in the swamp, slow but strong, capable of pulling as many as forty logs through the water to the sawmills.

In 1985, Latiolais and his brother Albert searched and found just one vintage bateau in all of Louisiana—one they had built. The brothers once hosted a ten-day boat-building demonstration at the Smithsonian Institution in Washington.

Tony and an apprentice, Danny Angelle, spent at least four hundred hours on the putt-putt bateau's construction in Butte La Rose. They searched the water for the visible ends of usable logs, marking them until low water when they could dig them out with shovels. Flagging the logs, it is called. Tony even wove the rope for old-style rope bumpers. The boat has a Model A gas tank. Every rib is a different length, and the work was painstaking and slow.

Tony takes his boat to Henderson Lake almost every warm weekend, effectively demonstrating why it's called a putt-putt. It moves like a string of firecrackers through the lake and canals. We used to see it—after hearing it first—from the *Green Queen*. It was one of the few loud noises I didn't mind hearing disturbing the swamp peace. Somehow a boat made with such loving care from logs left distressing in the swamp gave the sound an authenticity that a jet ski or air boat will never have.

My affinity for boats comes naturally. My father loved them, had a beautiful mahogany power boat that he used for fishing and skiing when we lived in Pensacola. He even shared ownership of a homemade barge with his best friend, Sam. So I was born floating about on some semblance of a boat and, regardless of economic circumstances, have managed to remain afloat. On a slow day from a low hammock I once tried to remember all the boats I'd owned during my adult life, a sleep aid that beat counting sheep. I lost track at twenty-three.

THEY SAY A SAILBOAT is the most beautiful manmade thing on earth. I agree. They are also the most liable to being dog-cussed. *The Windsong* was a small sailboat with a beautiful name and a rotten hull. Jimmy and I bought it in Meridian, Mississippi, after test-sailing it on a small lake. That short sail that sold the boat was the last voyage of the *Windsong*. The boat sat for months on its trailer perch in the small backyard of our townhouse apartment in Jackson. As Jimmy carefully pulled off suspiciously soft patches of fiberglass skin, the rotten ribs became obvious. Still and all, it was the first boat either of us had ever owned, and sea-worthiness isn't everything. Remove the rot and fix the rest was our mantra. That sad, peeling-away process continued apace until half a boat carcass replaced what had been the Windsong. The landlord got tired of the eyesore—I still think I know which neighbor complained—and evicted us. We threw good money after bad and stored ballast bars and engine parts in a rented shed. Eventually all that was left of a twenty-two-foot ketch would fit in the attic of our new rented house. After several more moves, the only thing left took up even less space: I kept a single brass cleat.

There would be yet another sailboat—*The Ernie Pyle*, bought with journalism prize money—which once served as free honeymoon lodging for young, penniless friends. The blue tape with which I spelled out "JUST MARRIED" never did come off the hull, insuring lots of winks and raucous greetings whenever we took her out.

Sailboats, however beautiful, depend on the wind, and there's always too little or too much. I was greatly relieved when we sold *Ernie* and inherited an old, stripped-down pontoon boat we called *Tsunami*. That basic barge made it all the way down the Tennessee-Tombigbee Waterway from Pickwick, Tennessee, to Mobile, and back, with six people aboard. The indestructible old Evinrude didn't care if the wind was blowing or not.

When I married Don, I knew I'd found the right man when he admitted his sailboat ambivalence. In his younger days he had owned a small sailboat that he occasionally stored at a friend's farm where one day he chained it to the trunk of a century-old tree. The ancient tree immediately fell during a wind storm, crushing the boat. The tree had been a veritable Rock of Gibraltar until it hooked up with a sailboat.

Yes, Don and I agree on sailboats, and are kindred spirits when it comes to all other boats. Otherwise a frugal, sensible man, he, too, can be had when it comes to a boat. We have skiffs, a couple of pirogues, a Winder canoe, his duck boat, and, until mooring fees put us out of the business at Pickwick, a pontoon named *The Yellow Dog*. I won't even get into the yard-art boats that are works in progress in both the Louisiana and Mississippi yards.

So I understand why a man like Tony, an artist, really, devotes so much time and energy to boat-building. Few things in life deserve the care and money we lavish on boats. That old saw about boats being the hole in the water where you throw money is true, but there's another way to look at that reality. Boats, if you think hard about it, are the same as spouses or mothers or best friends in adolescence, put on earth to break our hearts but worth an enormous amount of trouble all the same.

My Mabel

ohnelle has so many relatives we often get confused about
the crooked forks in his family live oak. Once, when I met
someone with the same last name, Latiolais (pronounced
Latch-oh-lay), I asked Johnelle if they were related.

"No, that's Jeanette's cousin," he said matter-of-factly. Huh?
Jeanette's maiden name is Melancon, but then she's also kin to
another branch of the Latiolais tree. With so few surnames in
circulation in Cajun Country, it gets rather complicated. I've
finally learned enough to stop asking Guidrys and Boudreauxs
if they are kin to other Guidrys and Boudreauxs. They probably
are, but never the way you expect.

Johnelle's late father, Nick, and his siblings were born on a
houseboat that floated on logs in the swamp. They lived near
the town of Catahoula, quite possibly the most beautiful and
authentic Cajun town left in America. Catahoula remains an
unspoiled paradise because it is far off the interstate and hard
to reach; until a couple of years ago the levee road you took
there from Henderson was unpaved. Cows grazed on either
unfenced side of it. If you pass through Catahoula, you have
to be going. I can only imagine how pristine and appealing it
was during Johnelle's boyhood. A lake is the centerpiece of the
town, and live oaks as big around as lighthouses circle it. Our
singer friend Hélène, another Catahoula native, has written

a song about the place: "Ma Belle Catahoula," "My Beautiful Catahoula." It is such a pretty song I always fight tears when she sings it.

We met Johnelle's father, Nick, but he already was old and ill so we barely got to know him. He spoke little English. It was one of many times we wished we knew Cajun French. Nick Latiolais had been a riverboat pilot and had stories to tell for those who took the time to listen—and who spoke his language. We spent more time with one of Nick's sisters, Johnelle's Aunt Mabel, pronounced in the Cajun as May-belle. The way the family always said it, the name had a musical sound, with the emphasis placed in a lilting way on the "belle" at the end. Nothing like the stark pronunciation you usually hear of Mae-bul. We met the aunt one day in Jeanette's kitchen when Mabel delivered a big Tupperware bowl of homemade pralines. "I let them cook too long," she said, apologizing for the most heavenly candy I have ever tasted anywhere at any time. That is one of the few Cajun artifices, apologizing for culinary masterpieces.

"Mais, non," Jeanette said. "C'est bon!"

Mabel beamed. She was a strong and devout woman in her eighties who never complained and kept a small altar in her bedroom closet. She told wonderful stories of growing up in the swamp. Sadly, Mabel died before we got to know her well. But her wonderful sense of humor and stories of survival made quite an impression. About that same time, 2001, we got a new puppy. A yellow Labrador retriever. For some reason, without much discussion and in complete agreement, Don and I started calling the puppy Mabel. Not Mae-bul, but May-belle. We had liked the woman and her musical name and were pretty sure the family wouldn't mind. This was, after all, such a beautiful dog.

WE ARE DOG PEOPLE. I have had more dogs than I can count on both hands and feet. Living at the end of a dirt road in Mississippi has added to our private canine population. People drop off puppies with such regularity we cannot keep them all. We try and find homes for the overflow. Mabel we paid for, which is something I've rarely done, something I sure don't need to do. I've always theorized that mutts have more sense than the purebred dogs, and I still think as a rule it's true.

I'd always wanted a yellow dog, though, probably because of the movie *Old Yeller*, which made me weep as a child. It was one of the first movies I ever saw. I remember leaving the theater in a trance, so accustomed was I to the happy endings of fairy tale bedtime stories and television sitcoms. The concept of fiction ending in death had never occurred to me, with the possible exception of Red Riding Hood's grandmother who was eaten by the wolf. *Old Yeller* made such an impression that I thought about it for forty years, and, as a grown woman, decided to rent the video and see if the movie deserved forty years of consideration. On second viewing, the movie was the most maudlin, cornball, chauvinistic thing I've ever watched; when the father, played by the Davy Crockett actor Fess Parker, leaves on an extended journey he puts the young boy in charge of the household, ignoring the mother and normal chain of command. Even so, during the scene at the end, when Old Yeller gets rabies and the boy has to shoot him, I wept again.

Then, adding to my yearning for a yellow dog, there is that wonderful Robert Service poem, "Yellow." I suspect educated poetry freaks don't think much of Service, the Yukon poet, or of rhyming poems generally, but I really don't care. Don has his master's in English and loves "real" poetry. He can be quite the snob about it, and late-night arguments usually end with me championing Tennyson or some other Texas Leaguer just to get a rise out of Don. That takes some doing. Once Don's brother's wife, rather pointedly I thought, observed, "If a person can't get along with Don, he can't get along with anybody." It's true. The few disagreements that do fester between us are more often about what I view as the rigid despots of classical taste. Why should some self-appointed committee of literary scholars decide what's good and what's not? At any rate, I rarely can slip sentimental verse by him, but even Don likes this little Robert Service poem, which dares to force "agog" to rhyme with "dog":

One pearly day in early May I walked upon the sand
And saw, say half a mile away, a man with gun in hand.
A dog was cowering to his will as slow he sought to creep
Upon a dozen ducks so still they seemed to be asleep.
When like a streak the dog dashed out, the ducks flashed up in flight,
The fellow gave a savage shout and cursed with all his might.
Then as I stood somewhat amazed and gazed with eyes agog,
With bitter rage his gun he raised and blazed and shot the dog.
You know how dogs can yelp with pain; its blood soaked in the sand,
And yet it crawled to him again, and tried to lick his hand.
"Forgive me Lord for what I've done," it seemed as if it said.
But once again he raised his gun—this time he shot it dead.
What could I do? What could I say? 'Twas such a lonely place.
Tongue-tied I watched him stride away, I never saw his face.
I should have bawled the bastard out, a yellow dog he slew.
But worse, he proved beyond a doubt that—I was yellow too.

In Dawson City one August we visited Robert Service's log cabin, and I half expected to see a yellow dog sleeping in front of the potbelly stove. I certainly could see a yellow dog snoring in front of our wood stove, or riding triumphantly in

our red Ford pickup. Something about the red and yellow—
Remember "catch a fellow?"—spun the color wheel in my brain
and brought to mind log cabins, virgin forests, or maybe an
isolated seashore. Perhaps I've perused too many L. L. Bean
catalogues, I don't know. My yearning for a yellow dog—for
the record—started long before the book *Marley and Me* and
the current stylish status of the Labrador. You can't swing a
cat nowadays without hitting a Lab in some tony catalogue.
At any rate, my nurse friend Bobbie Williams had a wonderful old Lab named Cody, a pup so placid you could prop your
feet on his back and rest your beer can on his head. Bobbie
alerted me when Cody's offspring was about to have puppies.
Cody would be their grandfather. And Cody was born to be
a grandfather—placid, sweet, attentive. The new litter was in
Tennessee, and though I drove up expressly to pick out a yellow
dog, the puppy I ended up choosing was whiter than she was
yellow. She was platinum blond, really, with velvety white ears
and the biggest webbed puppy feet I've ever seen. She would
have to grow into her yellow, if you will.

MABEL IS SPECIAL. ASK anyone but Johnelle. She's no smarter
than Barney, a wonderful mutt who saw me through three
moves and a divorce. I've had several dogs more devoted to me
than Mabel, who has an independent, almost cat-like reserve.
Only in the mornings is Mabel what you would describe as
affectionate. At night she's as grouchy as a tired old man. Our
dog Maxi, for instance, was a stray who lived to be petted, or
for any positive attention. She would stand by your chair till
the cows came home, hoping for a kind word or even a fond
look. Tiny Boozoo, our current pound puppy, would leap into
a furnace to save me if I were in danger. Mabel might call 911
if she weren't busy doing something else.

I don't know why my love for Mabel has surpassed any I've ever felt for a dog in a mighty long list of dogs. It has surpassed the love I've felt for almost any living thing, for that matter. It may be because I was working a lot less and doing that exclusively at home when she came to live with us at five weeks old. I had more time than I'd ever had before to bond with a baby, to watch her every move, as it were.

"We're her love slaves," Don declared one day as he jumped up from his chair to let her outside, and then back in, for about the hundredth time.

Mabel, believe it or not, began life as an outdoor dog, which is what both of us had always had before. I felt strongly about letting dogs stay outside in the years before Mabel; dogs were an essential part of the good life, but to keep both the humans and the dogs happy, the critters must remain outside—except during rare Southern freezes. So each cool night we fluffed bedding in the doghouse shaped like an igloo, and we said good-night to the tiny white spot that was Mabel. Maxi, still living at the time, was getting grouchy in her old age, and bit Mabel's ears with some regularity. We'd hear the pathetic yelps in the night, and I, of course, would run to the rescue. Mabel began spending the remainder of each traumatic night curled above my head on the pillow, a golden penumbra with a comforting heartbeat. This happened with some frequency. You simply can't throw your halo out the door the next morning. Mabel, somehow, little by little, had made the great leap to becoming an indoor dog, and she knew it.

Mabel loved to ride, which was good, considering it took eight hours to get from north Mississippi to Henderson. She'd curl up like a comma at my feet and sleep most of the way. When we'd reach the final leg of the trip, the causeway, she'd stir and seem to know we were close. I never could figure if it was the swamp smells, our excitement, or if Mabel was simply at the end of her rope, travel-wise.

Not everyone loved Mabel. In a wonderful little book called *PsychoTherapy for Cajuns* by Greg Guirard of Catahoula, the author discusses the prevailing Cajun sentiment about pets in the house:

> Whatever psychological aberration requires some people to allow dogs to live with them in their houses and even sleep in their beds, most real Cajuns are not afflicted with it. It disturbs me, on a certain level, to see dogs and cats mistreating people so cruelly, controlling their lives—you know what I mean . . . Cajuns love their dogs, but we live in a relatively mild climate—dogs can survive well outside . . .

The first day I met Greg he stopped by the front fence. Mabel and Boozoo began barking insanely, refusing to let the humans talk at all. I figured I had handed him a new chapter for his next book, or at least underlined his convictions. Our dogs do control our lives; I knew exactly what he meant. But only rarely does Mabel treat us cruelly. Usually she is a benevolent dictator.

Our buddy Johnelle subscribes to Greg's position. Johnelle takes it one step further. He has no use for dogs inside or out. The only time the proud Mabel cowers is when she hears Johnelle's voice.

I think it's a tidiness issue. Johnelle and Jeanette keep the cleanest house I've ever seen. And keeping a perfect house is impossible with any dog, much less Mabel, who sheds twelve months of the year. In March she does something the dog journals call "blowing her coat," an off-the-charts, super-shedding event. White hair banks like snow in the corner of every room.

Quilts and sofa cushions appear to be white velvet instead of their actual color.

All I know is Mabel is worth vacuuming three times a day, which is what you must do in March. She looks at you with worried eyes and you know that putting her outside for the duration would be the same as banishing a retarded child to fend for himself in the great outdoors. It just shouldn't happen.

BECAUSE HENDERSON IS IN such prime duck-hunting country, strangers quite naturally assume that a Lab might be Don's hunting dog. "Is that a good hunting dog?" they'll ask in innocence.

On winter hunting days when Don rises before dawn and leaves for the swamp, Mabel pulls herself on her belly from beneath our bed and jumps into the warm spot her "master" unwisely left. Then the two of us sleep soundly until some sane hour, say seven.

Mabel and I certainly are not adverse to a swamp adventure; we both love boat rides. We prefer them in the afternoons when the setting sun still shares some warmth and makes a spectacular backdrop for the cypress trees. We are not stupid.

Because of the delicious food, we all tend to gain weight during our Henderson stays, including Mabel. As she matured, Mabel began to have more and more trouble sliding into her favorite sleeping place beneath our bed. Don did what any obedient dog-person would do. He cut small wooden blocks and raised the bed. That night Mabel seemed as relieved as a vain woman who steps on the scales and is surprised to find that overnight she's lost a few pounds.

Like everyone else who spends much time in Henderson, Mabel has a nickname. The inspiration came at a gumbo supper at Mr. Doug's and Miss Emmeline's home. Emmeline for years had a fat rat terrier she called simply, "The Baby." They loved The Baby the way we love Mabel, to distraction. Emmeline broke Greg's rule about Cajuns and their outdoor dogs. The Baby ruled the roost. This night The Baby was sitting on its cushy throne in the kitchen while Mr. Doug made a gumbo. Yet every now and then, either Doug or Emmeline would go to the back door and yell, "Baby New! Baby New!" We were mystified.

Finally it was explained that there was a new addition to the Mequet family, a cat. They called it Baby New. New Baby.

Mabel became, at certain times when our love for her overflowed and simply required an endearment, Baby New. She answers to both names.

One week Johnelle was visiting us in Iuka when we realized that both Don and I had dentist appointments. One of Don's many good traits is his loyalty, in this case to a dentist he'd been seeing for over thirty years. Trouble is, this dentist practiced in another town, another state, actually. So every six months we drove two hundred miles round trip to get our teeth cleaned.

Johnelle would have to babysit Mabel. It wasn't his idea of a good time, and he wasn't my first choice for the job. There were no other options, however, and we all reconciled ourselves to the situation. We tore off toward the appointment, and Johnelle settled in for a day of letting a spoiled dog inside and back out again.

Naturally, sensing her advantage, Mabel seized upon the opportunity to run off. Johnelle, who knew he would face both my wrath and suspicions if anything happened to my precious dog, almost panicked. The poor man hollered and blew a whistle and stomped down the driveway fifty times. Johnelle, who seldom admits such things, told us in a still-breathless voice that he'd been certain Mabel was gone for good. He had the decency to know that wouldn't do, not on his watch. I think Johnelle and Mabel bonded on that day, so grateful was he when the prodigal returned before we did. We found them side-by-side on the sofa, Mabel licking Johnelle's chin, or trying to. She had converted the last holdout.

Harry, the Doughnut Bomber

I t's actually very nice to spend down time in a place where nobody reads my column. There's a certain freedom in it, a chance to be known for qualities other than the semi-marketable ability to turn a phrase. Plus, I never have to dress or wear makeup, fearing that I'll get stopped in the grocery store's produce aisle by a stranger who thinks he knows me from the awful mug shot that runs with the column.

"I read you every day, or some days, anyhow, when my wife buys the paper. I don't read you, really, but she does."

There's almost nothing you can say to newspaper columnists that will make them feel good about themselves or their work. Trust me on that. If you take the honest approach and say, "I don't agree with everything you write, but I read your column," it's as if you've gone to a great deal of trouble to damn with faint praise. If you lie, the columnist knows it. The best thing to do—unless, of course, you can quote by heart a passage from a column at least ten years back—is to keep quiet about what is, in essence, no different from factory work.

My closest Henderson friends have vague ideas about what I do for a living, and Jeanette and Johnelle, of course, have read a few of the essays that mention them or their family and friends.

Jeanette keeps an old copy of my 1987 column collection in her china cabinet. That's possibly the highest compliment anyone has ever paid my work.

In Henderson, mostly, I am just a curiosity, the wife of a Mississippi duck hunter, half of that couple of oddballs who spend part of their year in Louisiana. That allows me to be an anonymous observer, a fly on the wall, much better for column-writing than the rinky-dink quasi-celebrity status that attaches to a local columnist who lives in the city she's writing about. The nearest newspapers that carry my column are in Shreveport and Hammond, which might as well be a million miles away. People in Henderson read the *Teche News* or, in some rare instances, Lafayette's *Daily Advertiser*.

Despite all of that, Johnelle at some point got a sense of what I look for in column material—interesting people being at the top of the list. As generous with ideas as he is everything else, he started locating things for me to write about. And he was good at it. Not since my Tennessee friend Edwin "Whiskey" Gray ushered me through the hills and dales of Tennessee's Pickwick Lake area have I had such expert help. Johnelle knows people. And he had one ace in the hole. Nothing would do but I meet Harry Broussard, the Doughnut Bomber. You've heard of Lindbergh, Earhart, Yeager, the Red Baron.

Atchafalaya Swamp has Broussard, the Doughnut Bomber.

Harry once owned a local marina, but by the time I met him in 2000 he had sold it and lived in Lafayette. The former Vietnam helicopter pilot became a local legend and got the Doughnut Bomber sobriquet the old-fashioned way: He earned it. I was a little disappointed, I must admit, when Harry walked into Robin's Restaurant, our designated meeting place, in typical exercise togs and tennis shoes. He looked distressingly normal, like any other amiable oil-field supply salesman with an engineering background.

I had expected a different look—a crazy, big-bearded, swamp-rat look to fit a tree-tickling pilot who specializes in dropping garbage bags full of hot doughnuts at rental houseboats and marinas in the Atchafalaya. (The air-borne doughnuts always came from Meche's bakery in Lafayette, by the way.)

The whole Bomber business was born back in 1980 when Harry designed and built—at home, in his back yard—a forty-by-sixteen-foot houseboat he christened the *Henderson Queen*, not to be confused with our *Green Queen*. He used swamp salvage to build it, and a multitude of naysayers predicted the homemade boat would never float.

"It looked like the launching of the *Queen Mary*," Harry said.

The boat alone made Harry something of a legend, especially after they filmed a beer commercial on the *Henderson Queen*. "Then," Harry said with a grin, "*Penthouse* came along and took pictures of naked women on it." The naked women writhing for the camera within binocular view of the shore is a sight the local "birders" still rhapsodize about. We've been told Frank and Johnelle were fighting over Basin Landing's binoculars.

All that success with one houseboat encouraged Harry Broussard to build three more houseboats, which he rented to those who wanted to get away from it all. The original *Henderson Queen* eventually disintegrated from hard use and went back whence it came—the swamp. On top of the boat-rental business, Harry kept up his flying. In 1989 he went into the National Guard, which sent him to a two-week "map-of-the-earth" school, which involved extremely low flying. Interests merged. He used his low-flying skills and Piper Cub to thrill his houseboat renters, routinely dropping hot doughnuts to a waving, smiling, hungry and appreciative audience. He would first drop tennis balls to test the winds and assure a bull's-eye.

"I must have dropped two thousand dollars worth of doughnuts," he told me. Why? Because it was fun.

One day he bombed a houseboat that didn't know Harry or his drill. When he made his customary pass, Harry said, "They scattered like a bunch of birds." And when he made the drop, nobody waved or smiled, much less grabbed the bag full of doughnuts. A friend later told him that group of tourists was convinced they were witnessing a drug drop.

THE DOUGHNUT BOMBER EVENTUALLY sold his rental houseboat business and his airplane. But he didn't stop making waves. He built a sailboat that looks like a treehouse on a barge. His newest model of the *Henderson Queen* is a real dandy, too. Like the original, it's made of cypress knees and sinker logs and wooden pallets. It has a bug-proof screened room with two mattresses still in their plastic skins, two porch swings, and a hole in the floor for convenient fishing. Most of all, it has character. One year I took a photograph of the *Henderson Queen* for our Christmas card. I try to avoid saccharine subjects for my Christmas card, and the swamp boat was the perfect look. Don and I took his duck boat out to the *Henderson Queen*, and I hung a Christmas wreath on its door. The card was a big hit, but not with everyone.

"People will think that's where you live," my mother winced.

It wouldn't be bad, but Harry's not selling.

Harry's houseboats, in fact, are the look that visitors want to see when they come for a few days to "experience" the swamp. Nobody cares anything about seeing the big, expensive, vinyl-sided floating yachts with satellite dishes. You can find those at any marina these days. I know at Pickwick Lake there are boats that venture out only on Independence Day and Memorial Day; the rest of the year they are moored in expensive slips where potted palms and expensive rattan furniture make the docks look like somebody's living room.

No, the swamp pilgrim wants to see something more rudimentary and romantic. He wants to imagine himself fighting the elements, sharing a dock with an alligator and fishing through the floor. Harry's boats fill that need in all of us to build a treehouse, camp out in the woods, get out of sight of land, walk in the rain. We don't want to do these things every day, but the Atchafalaya has the ability to stoke up our juvenile fires, to rekindle the need for natural smells and sounds that is born in us. Progress, technology, civilization—they all join forces to kill off our yearning to be one with our surroundings. But, every rare once in a while, we remember.

Harry the Doughnut Bomber left more than bags of hot dough full of holes when he buzzed through the willows and made his dramatic drops. He left us with reminders of things we instinctively know but routinely forget: It's okay to be a little nuts, for instance, if you keep your flight pattern harmless. And derring-do is not limited by law to the young. Even in middle age you are allowed to take risks, as long as your arthritis isn't acting up. You can live on a houseboat in the middle of a swamp if that's what moves you. Nobody requires that you take out a thirty-year mortgage on a brick ranch in the suburbs. The money you earn is yours to spend—on rotten boats, travel to Timbuktu, or doughnuts for total strangers.

The Retiring Romeros

On one of my quickie tours customized for weekend visitors, I met the amazing Romero Brothers, which sounds at first blush like a circus act, as if sensational siblings were acrobats swinging from limb to limb in St. Martinville's majestic Evangeline Oak. Not even close. These elderly brothers were sitting quietly at attention in straight-back chairs by Bayou Teche. On a third chair, a box lid held down by a rock served as a tip jar.

Ophe Romero was ready to play the Cajun accordion, a concertina-sized instrument, and Lennis Romero the triangle. For a small tip dropped in the lid, the Romeros would crank it up and play a song. For a big tip, the Romeros would crank it up and keep it going until you got into your car and left. For no tip, there could be a short conversation but no music.

Ophe wore a big white cowboy hat and was the more talkative of the duo; he also did all the singing. He said he had grown bored after retiring from a life of sugarcane farming and wanted a hobby. Ophe, who did not remember exactly what year, started coming down to this famous tourist spot by the chocolate-milk-colored Teche. Each day he patiently sat near the legendary oak tree and sang for a steady stream of paying visitors. Lennis, who had retired at about the same time, quickly saw how much fun his brother was having, and soon enough he joined Ophe down by the wild elephant ears on the bayou's edge.

By the time I met them, the two had been performing for years and had not missed a day, Ophe said, with the exception of Sundays. On Sundays they rested. They had been written up about a million times in newspapers and magazines, many of them foreign, and had performed their way into several local television commercials and home videos. The music gig sure beat farming. And it was fun to meet people.

"Laughing keeps you from having strokes and heart attacks," Ophe said with conviction, but you could tell he had said the exact same words before. He pushed back his big hat and worked his mouth like accordion bellows in what amounted to a silent laugh. Baby ducks were waddling around his feet. The scene was like something from, well, a Cajun bank's TV commercial.

I walked over and conspicuously put a couple of dollars in the box lid. There was no lag. Ophe immediately started squeezing and singing, efficient as a jukebox. First he sang "Jambalaya," and then "Back Door." He liked it when I said he sounded like D. L. Menard on the latter—he didn't really—and so he sang some more of the same song. Lennis did his part for merriment-on-demand with the triangle.

The Romeros were not the best Cajun musicians I ever heard, not by any stretch, but they were available in the middle of the day when most of my visitors wanted to "get out and see something." They also were sincerely friendly and as colorful as it got. They always amused guests, who took countless photographs of the brothers and the historic venue. It was a no-brainer for my quick, superficial tour of Cajunland.

I must have chatted with the duo a dozen or more times over several years. No matter how often I stopped by, Ophe, the designated talker, would ask me my name and where I was from. He always expressed surprise when I answered, for simplicity's sake, "Henderson." I'd say "Henderson" and he'd say, "You don't sound like it!" Next time, it might be no more than a week later, we'd go through the same drill—the question, the answer, the surprise. It began to seem like part of a vaudeville act. Both of us laughed, anyhow.

One day I arrived, guests in tow, and found Ophe alone. Lennis, a tourist center employee told me later, was gravely ill. I had been afraid something was wrong and had avoided asking Ophe. I heard not too long afterwards that Lennis Romero died. The solo Romero act went on for a while, Ophe and his accordion, but somehow the music was sad now, like Porter Wagoner after Dolly Parton left Porter's show and his shadow.

After what seemed a short while—it might have been a matter of several months, even a year; as an itinerant resident I often lose track of the exact timing to things—Ophe Romero was missing, too. The same tourist office woman as before told me Ophe had moved to a nursing home and had been missing a lot of days by the bayou. An era had ended. Laughing, it seems, cannot keep old age and its health problems at bay on the bayou indefinitely.

I bought a print of the Romero Brothers painted by a local artist. In it the duet is together again, and in fine fettle, Ophe pumping those bellows and Lennis banging in time on the triangle. I look at it often and imagine they are playing "Jambalaya," the ultimate crowd-pleaser, for a group of outlanders just off a tour bus. Ophe will finish the cheerful song and look straight at me and say, "Oh, yes, you're that lady from Henderson."

It's not as much fun now to visit the Evangeline Oak, but I still do. For some reason I feel first-timers haven't been here unless they see the tree that might have been much like the one Evangeline could have stood by waiting for her lost lover Gabriel, if, she'd had one and if Henry Wadsforth Longfellow had ever visited St. Martinville and been inspired by the scenery, which he did not and was not. Anyhow, I force all my virgin visitors to go.

One spring day with my Mississippi friends Beth and Pat, we got lucky again. The Romeros had not returned, of course, but a large, dressed-up crowd had gathered at the spot where the brothers used to sit. Pink and white bunting was hanging from the benches and tree limbs. A wedding was about to start at the little gazebo next to Evangeline Oak.

When I'm in a pessimistic mood, I contend that the New South is nothing but the imaginary friend of a few progressive newspaper editors, or Ted Turner in a new hat. I fear nothing much has changed in the Deep South, where I've lived all of my life, except superficially. Hate wears navy blue blazers now instead of white sheets. As a young adult, I believed that once enough mossbacks had gone to their punishment, racism would end. Boy, was I ever wrong about that. The Grand Wizards have all morphed into Young Republicans. I also was wrong to believe that the South eventually would shed itself of racist politics the way a snake shed its skin. That didn't happen, either. Instead, national politics adopted the attitudes, techniques, and vocabulary of George Wallace and Ross Barnett. Dressed it up a little for the TV, changed some of the secret code to make it more politically correct, but kept the bottom line.

It's downright hard to be in a pissy, pessimistic mood, though, under a spring sky in St. Martinville. And the more I watched the scene unfold, the happier I became. The outdoor

ceremony we stayed to watch was New South if ever anything
fit that billing. The groom was black. The bride was white. The
crowd was equal parts of both races. A jet ski hummed by on
the bayou as the vows were said. (Not everything in a New
South World is perfect.) A baby with one of those garter-like
bands stretched around its bald head seemed to have something
to do with the featured couple. When I was a teenager, young
girls were sent away to have babies out of wedlock. Now they
pass them around at the wedding receptions.

In a lovely spot dedicated to romantic legend, where two
old men for so long had made jolly, if so-so music, a couple
of starry-eyed kids promised to love, honor, and cherish one
another, till death or ambivalence do they part. Against a lot
of odds, probably wearing rented tuxedos and something else
borrowed, they made a bet. And with their courage, I suddenly
felt fresh and ready to try new things. If, in the heart of Cajun
Country, we can celebrate a union that might have inspired a
lynching fifty years ago, maybe there's hope yet.

IN HIS BOOK *THE Cajuns: Americanization of a People*, historian
Shane K. Bernard relates the 1940 story of black accordionist
Amede Ardoin. One night, while performing, Ardoin com-
mitted the offense of wiping away his sweat with a handker-
chief offered by a white female. He was beaten severely, and
eventually died from his wounds. Bernard, however, goes on to
write that "... Anglo-Protestant enmity toward both Cajuns
and blacks created at least a modicum of compassion between
the two minorities ..."

And now, in the same land beneath the same oak trees and
the same brilliant sky, the races are amalgamating in a way to
make George Wallace spin in his Alabama grave. And the
world doesn't come to an end, and that blue sky doesn't fall.

Life goes on to a livelier beat. Whenever I get visitors as far as St. Martinville, we usually truck on south to Avery Island, not an island at all but a salt dome that goes eight miles deep. It was to this plug of salt that naturalist Edward Avery McIl-henny brought his talent and thousands of exotic plants in the late 1800s. And it was his father, Edmund, who first made the famous pepper sauce after the Civil War. Yankees ran the family off the island and destroyed their sugarcane plantation and salt business. When the McIlhennys returned, the only thing left growing were hardy pepper plants from seeds from the Mexican state of Tabasco.

I tell people to expect the unexpected. Avery Island is a hill in a swamp, with salt in the ground and a Buddha in the woods. Buddha is from the Tsung Dynasty and sits behind a red Shinto gate and a bamboo fence. The shrine is high above a mossy pond where you'd expect to see an alligator before your would an Oriental shrine. Some days, on Avery Island, you can see both.

Buddha belongs to the part of Avery Island the McIlhen-nys call Jungle Gardens. The entrance is a grove of majestic live oaks and hundreds of camellia bushes. It is a lovely place to get married or pose in your bridal gown—many do both— if you don't mind telling people that you got hitched where they make hot sauce. *We got married in a fever. Hotter than a pepper sprout . . .*

Edward McIlhenny the naturalist made several Arctic ex-peditions to study migratory birds. When finally he returned to Louisiana, he discovered a bird closer to home that deserved his attention. The snowy egret, which long had been killed for its beautiful plumage, was nearly extinct. The birds were giving their lives for the art of millinery.

McIlhenny found seven young egrets and built them an

elaborate nesting cage over a pond. He had seen one in India. The egrets have been returning to Avery Island every spring since. They say more than one hundred thousand birds fly home after wintering in Central and South America. The birds wading in the ponds of the Jungle Garden are more impressive than the golden Buddha Emperor Hui-Tsung built.

Besides touring the gardens, you can watch a film about Tabasco and march through the bottling factory. There's also a country store where thousands of items are emblazoned with the familiar Tabasco trademark. You can spend as much as you want on Tabasco underwear, dishes, cookbooks, pottery, chairs, trivets, ornaments, and neckties. A sample of Tabasco ice cream is free.

Tabasco is made of three ingredients: peppers, vinegar, and Avery Island salt. That simple recipe is deceptive, however, because the pepper mash is fermented and aged for three years. The aging process makes all the difference, and there is a difference in hot sauce. Tabasco is the best.

Whenever I escort my tour groups to Buddha, I get in a contemplative mood. I can't help but recount to anyone who will listen the life lessons of lovely Avery Island. When your sugar is wiped out by the enemy, do something creative with your salt. Protect the birds in your own back yard first. And, oh, yes, relish the unexpected.

Stormy Weather

When the names Rita and Katrina are spoken in one breath, as they so often are here, it sounds like a reference to a couple of cute young waitresses in the Waffle House at the interstate exit. They are cheerful, gum-smacking gals, who in their husky baritones begin on Monday to plan their weekends. They have tattoos that peek out on a lift of cleavage straining their brown uniforms. Rita and Katrina, the fun girls from Cecilia. I wish.

Nine years to the month after the wild boar hunt that first introduced us to Henderson, there was Hurricane Katrina. These days, all over the South, we think of life as Before and After Katrina—BK and AK, if you will. Not since the Civil War, the nation's bloodiest war fought mostly on Southern soil, has the region reeled, suffered, and rallied in such dramatic fashion. Life here AK has been like watching the acts of a Shakespearian play, a tragedy, of course. Katrina was both a predicted and unfathomable storm that, pardon the oratorical pilfering, will live in infamy. None of us could have imagined her power and its aftermath. And though technically we'd all read those enterprising newspaper and magazine stories about how New Orleans is essentially a big bowl that could be filled with water given the perfect storm, the actuality was not without surprises. For one thing, people trusted the levees.

We live in a world of televised hype, where "trained meteo-rologists" each hurricane season warn us of "monsters lurking off the coast" any time there's a summer squall. In a way, we'd unwisely become immune to warnings, shrugging off the hyperbolic chatter.

All of that would change, soon and forever, AK. After Katrina hit the Gulf Coast, we once again became believers in science and its trappings—in weather radios, portable genera-tors, cell telephones, electric lights, and running water. Katrina changed the southern coastline and hundreds of miles inland, even the few parts of it, like Henderson and St. Martin Parish, which escaped her direct wrath. You might have been high and dry in the South, but you were not untouched.

For several days before Katrina reached land, we sat in our back room in north Mississippi and watched the enormous blob that grew on the Weather Channel's map. Not once, but several times, Don phoned Johnelle and told him, first in a jocular voice and then with some urgency, to head north. "This is going to be a bad one," he said. "Come on up here, Thibodeaux."

It's hard to remember now, post-Katrina, that once upon a time people were nonchalant, pretty good at riding out storms, and that nine times out of ten you looked a little on the squea-mish side for leaving all your earthly goods in the rearview mirror and shelling out money for a motel room somewhere up the road. The last storm that had done much damage in Henderson was Hurricane Andrew, and that, for the most part, was manageable damage, or at least it seems that way AK. Utility sheds blew away, a few Henderson homeowners lost roofing tiles. In the world BK, a body living—as the crow flies—forty miles inland usually didn't look altogether crazy to batten down the hatches, huddle around a generator and stay put. Those who have not been part of a traffic jam leaving a coastal town cannot imagine the trouble it is to flee. For one thing, motel rooms—if you can afford one—fill quickly. After Katrina, I met two women evacuees, one from Ocean Springs, Mississippi, the other from Louisiana, who shared the last available motel room in Corinth, Mississippi, some eight hours north of the coast. There were thousands in the same boat.

But before Katrina, staying put was an option. Johnelle and his family made their decision to stay based on television predictions and prior experiences. They remained in Henderson, and they got lucky. Katrina's broad brush swept slightly to the east of Henderson, Lafayette, and the rest of Cajun Country. But then, weeks later, Rita hit. The Katrina images were indelibly etched in the minds of all of us, and the storm growing to the west of Henderson looked potentially like an even-nearer miss. This time we didn't have to phone and beg the Latiolais clan to head North. This time—After Katrina—Johnelle, Jeanette, their two sons, daughter-in-laws, and four grandchildren loaded up in two cars and headed to Iuka, an eight-hour drive from Henderson.

WHAT HAD STARTED AS a great adventure for the four children ended up as an exercise in tedium. They gratefully tumbled out of the cars and into our Mississippi hollow, migrant butterflies that have been flying over water and finally have a place to light. They ran and laughed and chased Mabel and Boozoo. Everyone visited the two bathrooms. Don took the kids and anyone else who wanted a diversion for a ride on the pontoon boat we then kept on Pickwick Lake. We cooked a hamburger supper and spread it picnic-style on the screened porch. The children loudly divvied up the beds and claimed spots to spend the night. The adults huddled around the Weather Channel, our new best friend, and watched with both great relief and sorrow as this time the hurricane wrecked lives slightly to the west of Henderson.

The next day, before the children had worked the kinks out of their legs and the complaints from their souls, the adults herded everyone back into their respective rides and pointed them south. No amount of wheedling could persuade the group to rest for another day in a hurricane-free zone. Not even the promise of another boat ride worked. They were worried about frogs thawing out in the deep freeze if the power had failed, about getting back to their jobs, about being stuck in horrendous traffic if they waited too long to return. Most of all, they were worried about the diminutive Latiolais matriarch, Johnelle's mother, Toot, who had refused to make the long ride and had stayed behind with a friend. In record time, six hours, they drove home.

The wicked duo of storms with waitress names had missed Acadiana for the most part—there was considerable flooding during Rita in several towns, including Abbeville and Erath—but now served as a kind of funnel for those escaping from both directions. Katrina evacuees came from New Orleans and the Mississippi Gulf Coast to our area. Rita refugees—"refugees" was not the politically correct word, but it seemed to me an apt one; people were seeking refuge from the storm and its aftermath—poured in from Louisiana's Lake Charles and Cameron and points West. Lafayette grew by an estimated twenty thousand people almost overnight.

For several reasons, we didn't go back south to the storm-ravaged coast until November, about two months AK. For one thing, Katrina refugees from Pass Christian, Mississippi, were using our Henderson house. Two days after Katrina, a friend had asked if a family who had lost their surfside dream home could hole up in our cottage in Henderson. We didn't hesitate.

It felt good to contribute something. Considering the number left homeless, it felt obscene to leave any shelter empty in the storm's aftermath. Johnelle and Jeanette, as usual, went over to see about things. They hurried to unlock our house and turn on air-conditioning and otherwise make welcome the family—a middle-aged couple, their daughter and the grandmother—that had lost everything. They were not destitute, anything but. Within weeks they had bought new cars and clothes and made contact with their insurance company. It didn't matter. In the days right after Katrina, you might be an indigent or a millionaire but you were helpless. There were no motel rooms available, no rental cars, no working cash machines, no cell phone towers. Nothing worked and, for once, for a short while, having money didn't change things.

The rich family was glad to arrive at our cramped cottage. They were glad to get to any place where the power was on, the streets were clean—well, relatively clean—and where you could buy a restaurant meal. They left only when Rita roared up from the west. Then our evacuees evacuated again, this time to a relative's house in south Mississippi that somehow had escaped destruction.

The Henderson Bible Church behind our house opened its doors to evacuees. For six weeks or more Pastor Soileau and his wife, with the help of other church members, cooked three meals a day for anyone who needed to eat. They even fed the family holed up in our house. The little cinderblock church was a temporary home to sixty people at one point, and not just those who happened by asking for help. The pastor aggressively checked local rest areas and truck stops for displaced storm victims, finding folks camped out in their cars or out of gas and money with nowhere to turn. Soileau found permanent housing for some, including a family from Cameron—a coastal town demolished by Rita. They became our neighbors. A young woman with three boys settled into a trailer at the end of Dupuis Street; her mother moved into a FEMA trailer in the church's cemetery next to our house.

KATRINA, AND TO A lesser degree Rita, were tragedies so big that you didn't really have to go to them. They came to you. Even in uppermost north Mississippi, the state parks around our town of Iuka were housing storm refugees in the weeks just after Katrina. An Iuka beauty shop operator opened her business and home to several stranded families. Parties patterned after bridal or baby showers collected household items for those who had lost everything. Benefit barbecues and concerts and dances were held each week. At first, for a few days anyhow, it seemed like all divisions of economics and race were blurred. People were joining forces to help those in need, no matter who they were. It was the silver lining to a mighty big cloud. Then, another storm began to brew.

Race, unfortunately, occasionally rears its ugly head in Henderson in ways that match its 1950s ambience. It's the ugly flip side of that '50s coin. You often hear racial epithets that haven't been common for a long time. Worse, when there's economic stress, you sense there's resentment and distrust on both sides. People began to worry aloud that black gangs from New Orleans would resettle in south Louisiana. Rumors circulated that evacuees were spending their FEMA money on false fingernails and new hairdos. The hazard was over; the harping began.

Scratch at anything long enough and you'll find a racial angle. Katrina was no different. The storm not only transformed the southern landscape. It divided people into camps. It went beyond those who were hit by the storms and those who were not. The aftermath also gave us two distinct types. People sympathetic to the storm victims. And those who believe the poor get what they deserve.

To add to the sadness of death and destruction, it became increasingly clear that many Americans treasure their own hides, the hell with everyone else. It's that old, wrong-headed belief that, in the U.S., anyone who works hard prospers. In this theory luck, of course, has nothing to do with prosperity. So you have the deserving rich. The rest, the hoi polloi, well, maybe they don't *deserve* to prosper. In the case of Katrina, some actually said, there was an inevitable cleansing. If the poor hadn't been so poor, they could have evacuated in time. They would have had cars and money in reserve for lodging in case of a necessary evacuation. It's their fault that they are poor, ergo they deserved to take their natural-disaster lumps.

I am sad to say there are those of my acquaintance, both in north Mississippi and south Louisiana, who subscribe to that latter position. They truly believe they somehow personally make the cut, have the right stuff, work harder, and live cleaner. They are righteously well-off because they deserve to be, and you can't convince them otherwise.

Tragedies often tear families apart, cause divorces and schisms that never heal. This great tragedy as well served to exacerbate political and philosophical positions. I found myself avoiding some who I knew disagreed with me about the plight of the hurricane victims. It made me rethink long friendships, something that mere partisan politics had rarely done. This was deeper. A lot of folks I knew and even loved somehow were able to believe that fate and its flood waters veered clear of the cautious and clever and washed away what needed to be washed away. I realized after Katrina I had not known the depth of their feelings, or of my own.

In the wake of that monster Katrina, it was almost too much to take.

Fit to Govern

ormer Governor Edwin Edwards is a Cajun charmer. You've no doubt seen him on the television news, taking the oath of office in both English and French. Whether leading a high-stepping delegation of oil men to the gambling tables at Monte Carlo, or serving federal prison time for racketeering, he pays his way in the public domain by being the third most entertaining politician Louisiana's ever seen. In any other state, he'd be an unparalleled Number One, no problem. Not here, not with Earl and Huey Long still bigger than life in the history books.

It was January 1984, when I met Edwin Edwards, Louisiana's first Cajun governor. Our meeting was long before the racketeering trial that sent him to prison; it was his unprecedented fourth term when the feds finally got him. We met in his temporary offices on the outskirts of Baton Rouge just before his third term.

This bright day he was riding high, full of life and ambitious plans. He was, in fact, leaving later that same week for France. Edwards would host a five hundred-member delegation to Paris and Monte Carlo, a trip designed to pay off his $13 million campaign debt. Tickets on the chartered jet cost ten thousand dollars, a price that included air fare, a black-tie dinner at Versailles, a cocktail party at the Eiffel Tower, and a special mass at Notre Dame. Anyone who was anybody in Louisiana was on that plane.

Edwards boasted that the biggest single political fund-raiser previously had been for Ronald Reagan, which had raised a paltry $2.8 million.

He was unlike any politician I'd ever met, so unabashedly spiffy and scrubbed he was hard to look at straight on. He wore a checked sports coat, an open shirt, and alligator shoes. It was if someone had taken the old model, navy blazer bureaucrat to a television show called "Pimp My Politician." He was well-mannered, attentive, even solicitous, and kept offering me things. Coke? Water? Tea? Edwards himself never drinks anything stronger than soft drinks, and to those he's addicted. I'd been told he washes his hands nearly as often as Howard Hughes. He washed them once before we began our talk. Then he settled down behind his desk and made time for a long interview.

"My father was a strict Presbyterian, very intelligent, with an absolute moral code," he said. "My mother was a Catholic who loved other people and who was always sympathetic. I think I got the best traits of both parents."

I've always hated that the man Louisianans put into office an unprecedented four times met such an ignoble end. I liked him, immediately and involuntarily. I liked him because he was as handsome as a male model and personally answered every reporter's phone call himself within fifteen minutes. And because he vowed never to take himself too seriously. I almost believed him that day when he kept insisting he was honest.

In one way, Edwards paid his dues. He picked cotton to pay for his college textbooks. He won his first election in 1954, a city council seat in his hometown of Crowley. When he first ran for governor, Edwards piloted his own airplane, a

Beechcraft twin-engine, and lit it in every burg in the state. He kissed babies and every pretty lady he could flush from the swamp. He spoke to audiences in both English and French, depending on the venue.

Edwards campaigned in both penthouses and Pentecostal churches. "Now you know you have more money than that," he once chided a reluctant supporter whose meager check he tore in half before a whole congregation. He seemed to fit in everywhere—at whorehouses and revivals. He was an admitted womanizer long before the world had heard of Monica, but then such things play better in St. John the Baptist Parish than Peoria. He admitted he liked to gamble, hunt elk, and flirt.

"To lose this election [speaking of his third gubernatorial one, when he handily beat incumbent Governor Dave Treen] I'd have to be caught in bed with a dead woman or a live boy," Edwards bragged shortly before taking sixty-three percent of the vote.

"Oh, sure, I said it," he told me when I asked about his braggadocio. "I said it on a day I was over-exuberant about my chances, and I didn't think about being quoted."

The state, for a long while, loved his style, his good looks, his pithy rejoinders. They laughed at his shaky reputation. One joke said Edwards was so slick he could sell paper to Xerox. Another said he planned to leave his body to "Charlie's Angels." When a Baton Rouge radio station parodied the popular song "Bette Davis Eyes" as "Edwin Edwards Eyes," it became a big hit. Between his third and fourth terms, Edwards himself cut an album of Cajun jokes and songs.

There were near scandals and investigations during his first three terms, but none stuck. Finally, accused of extorting pay-offs from companies that applied for riverboat casino licenses, Edwards met his Waterloo.

I WAS REALLY SORRY, not so much for Edwards, but for the state as a whole and Cajuns in particular. He had been a walking billboard for that joie de vivre we mere Anglo Saxons can only envy. He had it all—including, back in 1984 when I met him, presidential aspirations. He was intelligent, a progressive on race issues and extremely good at recruiting industry. Edwards cut a dashing figure and put to rest once and for all the myth that all Cajuns are illiterate hicks, backwards bumpkins. He was just about everything—including creative—that you dream of in a politician. And he was successful—until his hand, perpetually in the cookie jar, got so swollen he couldn't remove it quickly enough. Too bad, I say, since entertaining politicians are as rare as the bubblegum pink Roseate Spoonbill that nests in the swamp in the spring. During his federal extortion trial, I asked a Henderson friend what she thought about his downfall. "We've known he was a crook forever," she said with a shrug in her voice. "Why are they going after him now? He's an old man. The state will just have to pay for his nursing home."

I remembered that old bumper sticker from the Duke versus Edwards campaign: *Vote For the Crook. It's Important!*

I also had high hopes for the state's second Cajun governor, Kathleen Babineaux Blanco, a native of New Iberia. Another Democrat, she isn't as flamboyant or stylish or charming as Edwards, but I hoped that might be a good sign. Maybe she would be as organized, efficient, and businesslike as she looks. Maybe she exuded a more positive, if not as exciting, Cajun image.

During the campaign, Blanco seemed tough enough. Some pundits said she triumphed in a tight election because it was revealed, days before the vote, Blanco had a hunting license and her male opponent did not. Such a revelation might swing it in Louisiana, outdoor paradise.

Blanco trotted through her first year at a more-or-less steady gait. Nothing spectacular, no chartered jets to Paris. But no huge missteps, either. She chose the wonderful Cajun artist George Rodriguez of Lafayette to paint her inaugural portrait, replete with one of his trademark Blue Dogs. Edwards had been stylish; Blanco was tailored but ladylike.

Then came Katrina. All bets were off. Governor Blanco, on national television, did the one thing that female politicians must never do: she cried. She railed against the uninterested George Bush, and vacillated in public between losing her temper at the feds and giving in to her emotions. Her critics smelled blood and circled. A recall petition circulated. Her schoolmarm demeanor was mocked and ridiculed.

If ever there was a time to cry, a season to be sad, this was it. A man might have gotten away with heart-welled tears and petulant accusations. Edwin Edwards would have roared to the rescue in his own bass boat, probably, and rescued the pretty girls and perhaps a few floating pairs of Italian loafers in the process. Kathleen simply looked hapless, and sleep-deprived. She threw a few televised hissies. To quote again from the wonderful Louisiana novelist Rebecca Wells, she dropped her basket.

In the rough and tumble of politics, especially Louisiana-style, you have to expect with each new administration a few recall petitions, a few indictments, a scandal or two. It wouldn't be Louisiana unless some lesser official was indicted. Katrina knocked down everything in her path, including politicians—local, state and national. Still, I had hoped for a Cajun comeback in the political realm. It would have been especially sweet for a woman to make the books as both popular and honest, and a Cajun to boot.

"They'd criticize the Lord if He were governor," Jimmie

Davis had told me in 1998. I'd interviewed him for the Atlanta newspaper just before his hundredth birthday. He was not talking about Governor Blanco—this was six years before she was elected—but about his own critics who said, in 1944, that Davis was more interested in a showbiz career than in governing. He had left the statehouse long enough to film the movie *Louisiana*.

"It was for twelve days, and the only vacation I took my entire first term," he said.

DAVIS, LIKE EDWARDS, HAD undeniable charm. That's about where the similarities ended. The little town where he had been born ninety-nine years earlier, he told me, no longer existed. Beech Springs, it was, in rural upcountry Louisiana, land of pine trees and Baptists. I guess if you live a century, towns disappear. People, too. The old man remained quick with dates, quotes, names, and stories. Even in the Byzantine world of Louisiana politics, the story of Jimmie Davis is not your ordinary odyssey.

He had been a sharecropper, history teacher, hillbilly singer, movie star, and, of course, a politician. He's in the Country Music Hall of Fame, the Gospel Music Hall of Fame, and the Songwriters Hall of Fame. He made movies with Ozzie and Harriett Nelson, knew Babe Ruth and Harry Truman, raised old Earl Long's blood pressure, and once rode his palomino, Sunshine, straight up the steps of the Capitol building.

Eclipsing all his other achievements, Jimmie Davis gave the world a song that won't go away. Mothers rock babies to sleep with it, scouts sing it around campfires, Madison Avenue sells thing to its simple tune. "You Are My Sunshine" is part of America's musical history. And that was not his first or only hit. Davis had started out singing the blues, bawdy little honky-tonk numbers that political opponents later would embellish and try to use against him. There was "High-Geared Mama," "Red Nightgown Blues" and "Alimony Blues." Not bad for a boy who learned to sing at Solemn Thought Baptist Church.

"I never made more than twenty-four dollars a year off the blues," Davis said. So he abruptly changed musical direction. And it was a sentimental hillbilly song, "Nobody's Darling but Mine," that put Davis's singing and writing career on track. With the proceeds, he paid a debt, bought a farm, and a five-passenger Ford for four hundred dollars.

It was quite the largesse for a man who began life as a sharecropper's son, the second of eleven children. The first home he remembered was a two-room shotgun shack with no amenities, not even an outhouse. "There were plenty of woods, though," he deadpanned.

Davis hopped a freight for Louisiana College in Pineville, where he picked and sang on street corners to help pay tuition. Then he went on down to Louisiana State and got a master's degree, which he used to land a teaching job at a women's college in Shreveport. The story might have stalled there, but for Davis's Friday night gig at KWKH radio. He called himself the Dixie Blue Yodeler and sang in a style reminiscent of another Jimmie, Jimmie Rodgers.

It was 1934 when "Nobody's Darling" became a hit, and Davis was off to Hollywood to play a singing cowboy in B-movies. He kept writing—more than eight hundred songs eventually—but he modestly dismissed the work: "Most weren't any good."

In 1944, at the height of Davis's Hollywood fame, friends back home in Louisiana persuaded him to run for governor. Several factions were involved in refashioning state government in the years after Huey Long's death. Davis remember an early campaign stop at a Shreveport park:

"It was 5 P.M.," he said with certainty. "There were people all over the hill. I spoke longer than I should have, turned the world upside down, solved everyone's problems. Then a woman yelled out for me to sing 'Sunshine.' I told her, 'Lady, this is not a singing matter. Maybe we'll get together later and sing.'"

That night, Davis and his first wife, Alvern, sat up late talking, finally settling on a stump strategy. He would get a band together and blitz the state with a little talk and a whole lot of song. He avoided political virulence and spread sunshine. It worked. It worked so well it incensed his political foes. Uncle Earl called Davis "a clown," and A. J. Liebling wrote that the only things Davis openly opposed were subversion and juvenile delinquency.

Davis sang all the way to the Statehouse. His first term drew mixed reviews. By all accounts, he helped the environment and returning World War II veterans and left the next governor, Earl Long, a $30 million budget surplus. He became governor again in 1960, this time singing against the backdrop of racial politics. Davis led the segregation forces and called five special legislative sessions to try to avoid court-ordered school desegregation. He caught hell for building a new, milliondollar Governor's Mansion, though Davis himself only lived in it for one year.

Davis ran for governor a third and final time in 1971 and calls it his "greatest political victory." He lost. Edwin Edwards won.

THE MOST MEMORABLE THING to me personally about the long story I wrote after our meeting was the photograph. I had snapped one of Davis and a fan while we had lunch at a Baton Rouge steakhouse. I delivered the roll of film with the old man's picture on it to the photo department in Atlanta.

When the story ran, in a prominent place on a Sunday and a section cover, the accompanying photo was of a man I'd never laid eyes on, jauntily bicycling with a woman at his side. The middle-aged man was not the ninety-nine-year-old Jimmie Davis, past or present. The woman at his side was not Davis's wife, Anna. I never was sure where the photograph came from, who the people actually were, or what happened to the photo I made of Jimmie Davis.

Such is the newspaper business. Snafu City. Glitch Gulch. It'll drive you nuts if you let it. For me it spoiled the Jimmie Davis story, which I had taken great care in writing. I apologized in a letter and on the telephone for the error—to Davis, his wife, and all of his political handlers. I told them the truth, which was that nobody at the newspaper really knew what happened. But I was not invited to the hundredth birthday party.

Personal Notes

y family was a keyboard family. The same way certain adults drove Fords, others Chevrolets, my parents swore by keyboard instruments, not stringed ones. Nuts to catguts. And wind instruments—don't even mention it. A sax might lead to sex.

Not that any of us Grimsleys really played much of anything. My older sister and I took piano lessons for years and mastered a few recital duets. I can still hear the tune called "Country Gardens" and get the shakes. She tackled the more difficult bass half with some authority; I did a timid treble. At one point our hands crossed, adding a contortionist obstacle to an already overwrought performance. You could say my sister played a little piano.

Daddy, of course, played Webb Pierce records.

I begged to quit piano and take up guitar. Folk singing was beyond cool back then. But Daddy laid down the law. If I wanted out of piano lessons, I could take accordion. Those were my two keyboard options. It was 1965. I was twelve. We struck a deal. I chose the accordion, a pretty blue Italian one.

What girl could foresee the hellish halls of junior high and the torment of a tall boy named Zane Smith? From seventh through twelfth grade, Zane followed me with his long arms making exaggerated squeezing motions and his voice uttering a wheezing donkey's bray: "Um-ug. Um-gu." It was a great joke, all at my expense.

Then there was the curse of competence. As bad as I'd been at the piano, something about what the French call a "poor man's piano" came easily for me. I won second place in a local talent show playing the heck out of "Twelfth Street Rag." In one sense, my timing was perfect; in another, it was awful. Mine was the generation of Jimi Hendrix and Janis Joplin, neither of whom played the squeeze box or hung around with those who did. Guitars and rock were hot; accordions were Saturday nights at home watching Lawrence Welk. Or, as an Associated Press writer once analyzed it: "By then, the accordion was beginning to buckle under the weight of musical and social revolution."

In high school I bought a guitar with my own money and taught myself chords, enough to play "Blowing in the Wind" and "Where Have All the Flowers Gone?" I put my geeky accordion in the darkest corner of the closet where it would stay for the next few decades. I played occasionally, but only while alone or in the company of close, sworn-to-secrecy friends. Once, in the 1980s, I was short of cash and tried to sell Old Blue in the classifieds. There were no takers. Not the first call.

IN THE 1990S THERE were distinct signs of an accordion comeback. One company reported it sold twenty percent more accordions in 1998. Billy Joel and Paul Simon used accordions in hit recordings. Irish music became popular, and it features distinctive accordion parts. I heard faint accordion in more and more mainstream recordings, in the country music I loved, in television commercials and even movies. And it was about that same time we discovered Cajun Country, where accordion is a mainstay in the music. In Acadiana, the coolest, hippest, most admired musicians all play it.

The king of the Cajun accordionists, Reggie Matte, each year strolls casually onto the stage during the very last number of the Hank Williams tribute show. The crowd goes wild. Reggie's appearance is nonchalant, brief and brilliant. He works behind the scenes as sound engineer during most of the show, which, for some, doesn't really begin until Reggie finally makes an appearance on stage.

"Let Reggie loose!" Johnelle hollers with abandon. It is as if Reggie Matte is a beautiful, sedated tiger held in captivity, ready to explode into native fury at any moment given half a chance. Hire another sound engineer, for heaven's sake, and let Reggie steal the show. Let him loose!

The French groove on accordion, both in Louisiana and France. It was a thrill to discover that in France entire weekends in picturesque villages are devoted to accordion festivals. Same is true in Cajun Country. Mulate's hosts an annual accordion contest, and seldom do you see a Cajun band playing without an expert accordionist.

In the early 1900s the Monarch brand of German-made accordions was the preferred instrument. They were called "les tit noirs," meaning "the little black ones." They were smaller than some of the older brands and black with pewter trim, thus the name.

After World War II, the U.S. was cut off from the accordion supply when the East Germans ended up with most of the accordion commerce. That's when the Cajuns decided to build their own copies.

Cajun accordions now are all handmade locally. They are works of art. Some even have white crawfish painted on the black bellows. I think that was the final temptation, a hand-painted crawfish that grew to look more like a crab when the bellows were fully extended. In a weak if optimistic moment, I bought an accordion at the Breaux Bridge Crawfish Festival. It was used but still cost a hefty eight hundred dollars. All day long I circled the accordion tent, drawn like a preacher to fried chicken. I figured anyone who could play the piano accordion, as I could, certainly could master this smaller, simpler-looking Cajun cousin. I forked over the eight hundred without blinking—and a few dollars more for an instruction video.

The crawfish on the bellows is the symbol of Martin Accordions, operating out of Clarence Martin's general contracting business in tiny Scott, Louisiana. Clarence and his stepdaughter Pennye Huval work on the instruments whenever they get a chance, spending an average one hundred and twenty hours on each one. Melodeons, the precise name for the smaller accordions, come in single keys, same as harmonicas, and Cajun musicians generally select the key that best suits their voice. Most choose C, as did I.

Turns out, the piano accordion and the melodeon are two different animals. The Cajun accordion is in the harmonica family, with the push and pull of the bellows making two notes of one button. That doesn't happen with a piano accordion. You wouldn't think that small difference would complicate matters as much as it does.

"By the end of this video, you'll be playing right along at the intermediate level," video narrator Joe Rogers told me. Video Joe was sitting in front of a blue curtain in his home and first apologized for any technical deficiencies I might encounter while watching the film. It was I who should have apologized to Joe. As he talked about flappers and bellows and air buttons, I freaked. By the time he added "a little bit about music theory" and drew a diagram that looked like a baseball diamond, I lost all confidence.

Pretty soon I put the video away and tried figuring things out on my own. I labored over "Silent Night" until Don was longing for one, but I never got the hang of the instrument. It didn't matter. The Cajun accordion is a thing of beauty and a conversation piece. And there is something soul-satisfying about owning one, not to mention finally hanging out in a place where accordion is cool. You cannot imagine the delayed gratification. All the old stupid jokes about accordions don't make a lick of sense here.

Two musicians driving in a car run out of gas. They decide to walk to town to get more. "Are you going to leave your accordion in the back seat while we're gone?" one asks the other, who shrugs. When they get back with the gas, someone's left another accordion in the unlocked car . . .

Zydeco musicians use piano accordions like my old blue one from childhood. It's one of the most visible differences in traditional Cajun music and zydeco, that and the fact that most Cajun bands are white, and zydeco bands black. The zydeco kings are strapped beneath the weight of a full-sized accordion, wearing it almost like a long-ago warrior wore breastplates to battle. They are proud, so proud, of the instrument I hid in the closet. They wear their music on their puffed chests, and it is regal.

The whole accordion saga, its ebb and flow, in and out of fashion, old-fogy or new age, reminds me of the patterns of style in life itself. None of us can hope to be current and hip constantly. Take hair, for a lowly instance. My timing wasn't so hot in that department, either. I came of age when surfer girls with long, straight, blond hair were all the rage. Mine is wavy and dark, more the 1940s' look. So, as a teen I did the only thing I could do. I ironed it. Conformity at any price. When you're hot you're hot. When you're not you're not.

I took the Louisiana popularity of the accordion as a sign I'd landed in the right place. The planets had finally aligned. If only my junior high tormentors could see me now, proudly shaking my curly head in time with the celebrated Cajun accordion players. Not out-of-step, not cutting edge. Mainstream, for once.

EVOLUTION. YOU CAN WATCH life begin each morning in the swamp. If you insist on compressed creation, this is the place. And you don't need the full seven days an evangelical's world premiere would require. It can happen in that few minutes between the rosy-fingered dawn and full light. It's a time-lapse snapshot of billions of years, unfolding in seconds as witnessed from a johnboat.

Something begins to bubble beneath the green carpet of hydrilla, unseen proof of life. Something else, a nutria or muskrat, slithers from water to land with a beginner's grace. There's movement in the tall grass. A heron with awkward legs crashes about at the edge of the Atchafalaya. A turtle plops from a log with a satisfying splash. A mosquito screams in your ear. The snowy egret dangles from a willow limb like a boll of unpicked cotton. An owl hoots a confused hello. The swamp teems with life, not static, almost electrified.

You also see the big tracks of Homo sapiens—abandoned pipe lines and litter and oil streaks across a bayou's slick surface. The connection between our species and all the others is never so clear as while floating on Henderson Lake in early morning light. We are a higher species with low-down habits. And all of us still have mud on our backs.

The appeal of the swamp is visceral, changing somewhat

with the seasons, altered occasionally by man, yet constant. It's the same as what Jacque Cousteau once said about the ocean: *"The greatest resource . . . is not material but the boundless spring of inspiration and well-being we gain from her."*

Don remembers why we love Louisiana when I forget. He is in the swamp a lot more than I am, and the swamp is everything. Whenever I need a reminder, we go for a long boat ride. That's all it takes. The house, the azaleas, the accordions—all are nice but not necessary. Not vital. The Atchafalaya, on the other hand, is the link between yesterday and today, the bridge between primordial goo and advanced civilizations. Like California's redwood forests or the ocean, there is implied history in the look and smell of the place, a remembrance of what used to be and could come again. When the genius Mississippi artist Walter Inglis Anderson camped beneath his overturned boat on the barrier island called Horn, studying the light and the critters and the movement of the tides, he lived without technology. He left on the mainland his gun and gig, opting for oars and sail instead of an outboard to get to the island. He had the right idea.

We are not the purists that Walter Anderson was. We use a motor to get about in the lake, and we certainly don't stay all night beneath our boat to battle the mosquitoes and elements. But we do share Anderson's admiration of the natural world. Few places are as stunningly untouched by humans as the Atchafalaya.

EVERY NOW AND THEN, Don or I will stare incredulously at the tax or insurance bill that's just arrived in the mail and say with a concerned frown but no conviction: "Maybe we should sell the Henderson house. We just can't afford to keep up two homes."

The Devil's advocate—I'll admit, it is usually I—holding the bill will wait for a response. It is always forthcoming. The other person will recite a long list of reasons we cannot live without our Louisiana residence. Each time there's a necessary belt-tightening, something else gets eliminated. We have sold a pontoon boat—and it's not like us to sell a boat—upped all our insurance deductibles, cut down on trips to France and to town. We shop for bargains at the bent-can store. We have slashed at luxuries as if they are attacking serial killers. But we can never conclude—at least not both of us at the same time—that the Henderson home is a place that has to go, one we cannot afford to keep. It is not a luxury, not really. It's a limb, and we are loathe to lose it. Someday, for financial or health considerations, we may have to make a decision and choose one home over the other. It will be a sad day, or a cold day in Henderson.

We have settled into a satisfying pattern during our stays in Atchafalaya Swamp. It might rightly be called a rut, but for all the fun. Don hunts most weekday mornings during duck season, of course. He avoids the crowd and lets those not yet retired have the weekend fun. I am mostly content to play in the house and the yard and occasionally get some writing done. Together we explore, entertain, eat too much. We live full lives in more than one sense. The dogs are there, of course, getting fat along with us. We no longer go to large festivals; again, that seems best left to younger folks, whose time is more limited than ours. They need the fun and food in concentrate. We, however, hear a lot of good live music at small local restaurants and clubs and, once or twice a year, at the Eunice theater. Because all the most important holidays fall during duck season—you notice I did not say that duck season occurs during the holidays; passionate hunters consider it's the other way around—we have been in Henderson almost every Thanksgiving and Christmas for a decade.

FOR THE LAST FIVE or six years, we might as well have been named Latiolais. We take Thanksgiving and Christmas meals with Johnelle and Jeanette and their extended family, at their insistence and with great enthusiasm on our part. Throw in Johnelle's New Year's Eve gumbo, and you might say we've eliminated the pain of holiday cooking. I do next to none. Why would I? Cooking for ourselves when we've been invited to the Latiolais house would be like making a peanut butter sandwich and sitting curbside in front of Brennan's to eat it.

"Boudreaux. Gumbo's ready," was the message Johnelle left on our answering machine one day. We kept it on the machine for at least a year. Somehow that said it all.

Jeanette's holiday meals start at noon or before, and usually several shifts are involved in the seatings. She has a big dining room table, but not big enough. Her stove top and counters are laden with three or four kinds of meats, each so expertly seasoned and cooked that you sometimes don't recognize her version as meat you've ever had before. Jeanette's pork roast, for instance, is nothing like one of the thousands I've ever cooked. I would swear it's not from a pig at all but some heavenly hybrid. There are at least two big pots of white rice, mounds of it. Everyone who comes to eat brings a dessert—we have to do something—so one end of the long counter looks like a branch of T-Sue's.

Gift-swapping usually happens on Christmas Eve. It reaches a crescendo when Johnelle's mother, Toot, arrives. She ceremoniously gives each child and grandchild an envelope with money, and there are pleased exclamations all around. You must collect in person; that's her only condition. You don't show up, you don't get your money. And then, after the money envelopes are passed around and admired, bedlam ensues, as children and adults alike tear into pretty packages simultaneously, briefly turning Jeanette's perfect house into a department store with inventory by A-bomb.

Despite our protests, we get lots of gifts, too, mystery packages from Jeanette and Johnelle and their sweet, giving children. If anyone resents us being at each and every family scene, they hide it well. We are treated like family, and—in this family—that's an incredible thing.

Each warm and wonderful holiday season I can't help but remember that first Christmas on the *Green Queen* when I felt a little lonely and outcast. I remember I actually worried we would never feel a part of this community. What, in heaven's name, were we doing here? How things have changed in ten years. Not only do we feel a part of the community. We have been adopted by a bona fide Henderson family, and are accepted and loved for ourselves. The only time I can remember Jeanette and Johnelle getting cross at me is when they thought I waited too long to telephone them about Don's heart bypass surgery. Why hadn't I called them right away, soon as we knew? After all, they said, you are family.

The memories are like the intimidating trunk of photos in the Henderson attic. There are so many it takes too long a time for sorting. Best just to keep making new ones.

CHANGE IS INEVITABLE, OF course, even in Cajun Louisiana, where both geography and strong sense of community for so long have kept cultural distinctions pure and alive. What once was a rural scene inextricably linked with the woods and the fields and the swamp is becoming more urban with each passing day. Even in our Henderson, where most still make their living either directly or indirectly from the Atchafalaya, things are fast evolving. Each time we're away for a couple of months, another new subdivision sprouts in a former sugarcane field. The back road between Henderson and Breaux Bridge is filling with large brick houses, nothing like the little frame ones we first admired. Beneath interstate billboards advertising "Vasectomy Reversals," the population grows and grows.

The recreational boats seem to outnumber the work boats on Henderson Lake these days, especially on the weekends. Not too long ago they paved the dirt road along the levee between Henderson and beautiful Catahoula. It takes a fourth of the time to drive between the towns now and your car stays clean, but you no longer have the bucolic sightings of free-range cows and carpets of wildflowers. There's a never-ending assault on the landscape from twenty-first-century technology. There are more cell towers in the vacant lots, more wide-screen televisions in the living rooms. You see ATM machines in grocery stores and, all around, other effluvia of a whiz-bang age.

A Wal-Mart Super Center is going up in neighboring Breaux Bridge, and already a McDonald's and a Popeye's have joined the phalanx of gas stations at the Henderson exit at the foot of the long causeway bridge. Henderson Cajuns un-self-consciously rush through the drive-through at Popeye's and order their red beans and rice. You can run from progress, but you can't hide.

The food and music that this place not so long ago exported has boomeranged back in the oddest of arrangements. And while the Cajun craze shows no sign of abating—Don and I saw a Cajun restaurant on our tour of Alaska—the culture's popularity is paradoxically cheapening it. Anyone with a red pepper shaker can call his food Cajun and fool those who have never had the real McCoy. Cajun dance clubs and dance halls are in Atlanta and Birmingham, employing Cajun musicians but relocating them as well. Today you can buy a generic king cake in the Krogers of Mississippi's nearly unanimously Protestant hill country.

WHEN I TRY TO explain my fascination with Henderson, it always comes back to the people. They are what makes the area unique and will continue to do so whatever the superficial scene. The Cajun culture may not remain pure, but the Henderson heart will. There is a real distinction in the spirit, the generosity, the unpretentiousness of those we have grown to love here. They are old-fashioned in the best sense of the word. Johnelle may have a cell phone constantly to his ear, but he's using it to arrange a favor for a friend. Jeanette may use a computer to rent out movies to customers at the M&M, but she retains a true sense of pride in family and a job well done. They do not qualify friendship. They are what Willie Nelson calls *good people,* as dependable as sunrise and sturdy as cypress planks. They are the friends I would call in an emergency, or to celebrate an achievement, or to help bury my dog. They would be there, in an instant, with medicine or money or a strong back. They give because it is part of their nature, same as breathing or sleeping. They help one another because survival has taught them how.

I don't pretend to have significant insights into the culture called Cajun. I wouldn't call my experiences typical, or even representative. Henderson is a small if significant dot even on the twenty-two-parish map called Acadiana. Those with more scholarly credentials will have to make the sociological calls necessary to explain a people. Yes, they are the descendants of the original Acadians, dispossessed and driven from Nova Scotia by the British. Beyond that, the Cajuns I love defy sweeping definition or description. They are individuals in the truest sense, my giving, funny, irrepressible friends. They are noble.

I profess to know only what I have seen and heard in an unforgettable decade of living amongst my Henderson neighbors. I've really learned more about myself than I have the Cajun people. I'm happier—better, if you will—for having found Henderson. You might say I've learned *from* my friends, not *about* them. I have been privileged, I know that much. I've seen exotic sights in an ordinary town, met unforgettable people in a workaday world. I've heard incredible music from porch steps and stages, eaten food from paper plates that would please a king's palette. I have floated about the dark waters of another time, remembering things I never knew I knew. I have learned to love children and a culture that are not my own, telling them good-bye whenever our time was up and it became necessary. I have laughed, cried, eaten too much, spent too much, given alligator tours, and learned to make a roux.

I am not from around here but I intend to stay.